THE WORLD
OF THE
NEW TESTAMENT

THE WORLD
OF THE
NEW TESTAMENT

Edited by

JAMES I. PACKER, A.M., D.PHIL.
Regent College

MERRILL C. TENNEY, A.M., Ph.D.
Wheaton Graduate School

WILLIAM WHITE, JR., Th.M., Ph.D.

THOMAS NELSON PUBLISHERS
Nashville • Camden • New York

Published in Nashville, Tennessee, by Thomas Nelson,
Inc., Publishers and distributed in Canada by Lawson
Falle, Ltd., Cambridge, Ontario.

Printed in the United States of America.

Library of Congress Cataloging in Publication Data
Main entry under title:

The World of the New Testament.

    Includes index.
    1. Bible. N.T.—History of Biblical events.
2. Bible. N.T.—History of contemporary events.
I. Packer, J. I. (James Innell) II. Tenney,
Merrill Chapin, 1904-   . III. White, William,
1934-   .
BS2410.W68 1982   225.9'5   82-12548
ISBN 0-8407-5821-9

TABLE OF CONTENTS

INTRODUCTION

The World of the New Testament provides information about the immediate background of New Testament times and the situation in which it was written. The New Testament was not created in a vacuum. It was, rather, written following a long history of God's dealings with Israel. A knowledge of that history will help us to understand the New Testament more clearly. For instance, the New Testament's teaching about salvation cannot be understood unless one is familiar with the creation and fall of man; the teachings of Christ are best studied in the law of Moses; and the person of the Messiah must be considered in relationship to David and the promises which were made to him.

In *The World of the New Testament* the history of the New Testament period is viewed from the perspective of how it affected New Testament events. This history extends back to the intertestamental era since its events influenced the New Testament world.

The study of chronology—the dating and proper sequence of events—is also vital to a proper interpretation of the Word of God. We have dealt with this subject in some detail in this volume. The Greeks and their program of Hellenization helped set the basis for the culture of the New Testament era. Many of the conflicts and struggles that existed in the days of Jesus and the Church were consequences of the rule of Alexander and his successors. The Romans influenced the immediate situation. As they controlled the government and the economic strings of the nation, they also affected the cultural and religious practices of the day.

A knowledge of Jewish customs and practices aids our understanding of the conflicts that Jesus encountered during His ministry. Because Jesus' conflicts with the Pharisees play such a prominent role in the Gospels, it is surprising to some to discover that many of the factions and sects of Judaism were

very unlike the legalistic Pharisees and had a spiritual understanding of the Law.

The chapters devoted to Jesus, the apostles, Paul, and the
early church bring together the historical facts recorded in
the New Testament. Since these facts are frequently scattered
throughout the New Testament, we believe that many readers
of the Bible would find their orderly presentation most
helpful.

The *World of the New Testament* should be a useful reference
book. The student of the Bible is urged to make this
handbook a companion volume for the study of the New
Testament.

1
NEW TESTAMENT HISTORY

The story of the New Testament began long before Jesus was born. In fact, many of the incidents recorded in the New Testament can be understood best only when that long history is known.

It begins with the creation of the world—including Adam and Eve, the first man and woman. When they sinned and disobeyed God's command, the perfect environment in which they had been created became flawed. And so the story of God's redemption of mankind—which culminated in the life, death, and resurrection of Jesus of Nazareth—begins.

This story continues with God's call of Abraham sometime around 200 B.C. Abraham was called to leave his home, to travel to a new land, and to become the father of "a great nation" (Gen. 12:2–3)—Israel.

Within a relatively short time, however, Abraham's descendants found themselves in Egypt. Soon their number became a threat to the pharaoh—the ruler of Egypt—and he ordered that they be made slaves.

It was during this time that Moses—the most crucial person in Old Testament history—was called to lead Israel out of bondage in Egypt to the Promised Land of Canaan. Following the exodus from Egypt (near 1450 B.C.), Israel received the Law—the laws and social institutions that were to be observed in the new nation, including the Ten Commandments. When the fearful Israelites refused to enter the Promised Land as God commanded them, the Lord condemned them to wander in the wilderness area south of Canaan for another forty years.

It was Moses' successor, Joshua, who led Israel into the Promised Land. This conquest was a violent time—the Book of Joshua tells the story in detail.

Following Joshua's death, ". . . every man did that which was right in his own eyes" (Judg. 21:25), and it was necessary for God to raise up judges. These colorful figures called the people to repentance and defeated Israel's oppressors—the Book of Judges tells their stories.

Saul was Israel's first king. His successor, David, chose Jerusalem as his capital, making it both the political and spiritual center of the nation. David's son, Solomon, succeeded him. Solomon consolidated his father's kingdom and built the great temple in Jerusalem. Known for his great wisdom, he was also a foolish leader; his love for luxury, beautiful women, and political alliances had a disastrous effect on the nation.

Following Solomon's death a bloody civil war ensued, with the nation splitting into Israel in the north and Judah in the south. Both Israel and Judah fell into idolatry and sin, and God raised up prophets—men who declared the will of God to His people—to call them to repentance. Both nations

Ephesus. Paul visited the seaport of Ephesus on his second and third missionary journeys. A major landmark of the city was this theater, which the Romans built to seat about 25,000 people. In this arena the silversmith named Demetrius led a riot against the Christian evangelists (Acts 19:24-29).

ignored the prophets' warnings, and ultimately both were destroyed by their enemies—Israel by Assyria in 723 B.C. and Judah by Babylonia in 586 B.C. The leaders of both nations were taken captive and sent into exile.

Later, many of the exiles' descendants returned to Palestine. One group returned in 538 B.C. and rebuilt the temple; another returned in 444 B.C. and rebuilt the walls of Jerusalem under the leadership of Ezra and Nehemiah. Israel's old pattern of slipping into sinful practices and indifference reappeared; and with the close of the Old Testament period, we hear the voice of the prophet Malachi condemning their sinful ways.

THE INTERTESTAMENTAL PERIOD

The four hundred years from Malachi's writing to the coming of Christ are known as the Intertestamental Period. The books of the Maccabees, which describe the Maccabean revolt and the chaos in Palestine, and the writings of Josephus, a first century A.D. historian, are the chief sources of information for this period.

The Book of Daniel gave a preview of these years. Through the eye of prophecy Daniel was able to outline the major political events of this time. Daniel lived during the ascent of Babylon as a world power. He saw that kingdom pass off the scene to be replaced by Medo-Persian rule. In his prophetic vision then, Daniel saw the rise of the other great powers that would dominate the period between the testaments: Alexander, the Ptolemys of Egypt, the Seleucids of Syria, the Maccabees, and the Romans.

A. The Later Persian Period (through 331 B.C.). The Old Testament closes with the Persian Empire still in power. Cyrus had allowed the Jews to return to the land to rebuild the temple (538 B.C.). Esther, a Jewess, had risen to prominence in the palace of the Persian king (470 B.C.). Ezra (456 B.C.) and Nehemiah (443 B.C.) had returned to the land and had instituted their reforms.

Nothing of much international political interest happened in Palestine during the remainder of Persian rule. The Jewish high priest governed the land, and the office became a highly coveted one. Several disgraceful contests for the position took place. On one occasion a high priest killed his brother when he sought the position for himself. The Persian governor was so appalled by this act that he imposed a heavy fine on the population.

B. The Period of Alexander the Great (335–323 B.C.). Persian rule was followed by Alexander's rise to power over a vast empire, including Palestine. Philip of Macedon, his father, had extended his rule over all Greece and was preparing for a great war with Persia when he was assassinated. His son Alexander, only twenty years of age, succeeded him and within a short time cut the power of Persia to pieces.

In 335 B.C. Alexander began his memorable reign of twelve years. After establishing his rule in his homeland, he marched eastward conquering Syria, Palestine, Egypt, and eventually Persia itself. He sought to conquer lands further east, but his troops refused to extend themselves any more. He died in Babylon in 323 B.C. In his thirty-two years of life he made an indelible mark on history.

C. The Era of the Ptolemys (323–204 B.C.). No one rose to succeed Alexander. Eventually four of Alexander's generals divided the empire. Two of them, Ptolemy and Seleucus I, would be involved in the rule of Palestine.

After some struggles among these generals, Egypt fell to Ptolemy Soter. Palestine was also added to his share. At first Ptolemy Soter was harsh toward the Jews. Later, he used them in various parts of his kingdom, often in high offices.

His successor, Ptolemy Philadelphus, was one of the most eminent of the Ptolemys. Friendly to the Jews, he promoted the arts and developed his empire in all respects. The Hebrew Scriptures were translated into Greek during his reign in the Egyptian city of Alexandria. The Septuagint, as this version was called, could then be read throughout the empire.

In time, rivalries developed between the kings of Egypt (the

Ptolemys) and the kings of Syria (the Seleucids). The rivalry came to a climax during the reigns of Ptolemy Philopater (222–204 B.C.) and Antiochus the Great of Syria (223–187 B.C.). Philopater was able to conquer Antiochus in a battle near Gaza. On his return from the battle, Philopater visited Jerusalem and determined to enter the Holy of Holies in the temple. Though the high priest tried to dissuade him, he made the attempt. Josephus reports that when he got as far as the Holy Place, he was seized with such terror that he left the temple.

Because the Jews had opposed him, Philopater withdrew their privileges, fined them, and began to persecute them harshly. Rounding up all Jews in Alexandria he could find, he locked them in a hippodrome filled with drunken elephants. He expected them to fall on the Jews, crushing them. Instead, the enraged elephants escaped, killing many of the spectators. Philopater took this as a token of God's favor toward the Jews and ceased persecuting them. At his death in 204 B.C. he was succeeded by his son, Ptolemy Epiphanes, who was only five years old. Antiochus the Great of Syria took this opportunity to wrest control of Palestine from Egypt.

D. The Syrian Period (204–166 B.C.). The Egyptians sent an embassy to Rome asking for their help against Antiochus. Agreeing to this request, Rome sent an army, although it was initially unsuccessful. Eventually, however, they forced Antiochus to evacuate the whole country west and north of the Taurus mountains. On a raid in the east to finance his war, Antiochus was killed by the inhabitants of the province of Elymais while plundering a temple of Jupiter.

The reign of his successor, Seleucus Philopater was uneventful. But with the rise of Antiochus Epiphanes ("the manifestation of God"), one of the darkest eras of Jewish history began.

Onias, a worthy man, held the priesthood in Jerusalem when Epiphanes began his reign. Because the Greeks desired to Hellenize the Jews, Epiphanes sold the high priesthood to the brother of Onias for three hundred sixty talents. Onias fled the city. The usurper changed his name from Jesus to Jason, thus collaborating with Antiochus' effort to impose Greek culture and religion on the Jews. Old Hebrew customs and religious practices were discouraged; Jews were sent to Tyre to take part in games in honor of the heathen god Hercules; and sacrifices were offered on his altar. Eventually, Menelaus, another brother, outbid Jason for the priesthood and intensified the attack on Judaism.

When Antiochus Epiphanes went to Egypt to quell an uprising, a rumor that he had been killed was circulated and the Jews began to celebrate with great joy. When he heard of this, he returned to Jerusalem, besieged and took the city, and massacred forty thousand Jews. To show his contempt for the Jewish religion, he entered the Holy of Holies, sacrificed a sow on the altar, and sprinkled the blood all over the building. At his command the temple became a temple of the Olympian Zeus; Jewish worship and sacrifices were prohibited; and pagan rites were substituted. Circumcision was prohibited, and the mere possession of a copy of the Law was made a capital offense.

The Jews resisted. One man named Eleazar, an aged scribe in high position, was killed because he would not eat swine's flesh. One after the other, a mother and her seven sons had their tongues cut out, fingers and toes removed, and were cast into a vessel boiling over a fire. One body of resisters, numbering about one thousand, was attacked on the Sabbath. Refusing to break Sabbath prohibitions, they were put to death without a fight.

A family of the priestly class called the Hasmoneans force-fully resisted the edicts. When the emissaries of Syria attempted to enforce the edicts of Epiphanes, Mattathias, the father of the family named the Maccabees, refused to worship the pagan gods. When another citizen presented himself at the altar to sacrifice to the heathen gods, Mattathias killed him. He then led a band into the wilderness area where David had eluded Saul for so many years.

Gradually the number of those standing with the Macca-

Antiochus III. This Seleucid king took Palestine from the Egyptians in 198 B.C. But the Romans subdued Antiochus in 190 B.C. and seized much of the territory he had conquered.

bees increased. The Syrians launched three campaigns against these faithful Jews, one by Antiochus Epiphanes himself; but none were successful. In time, Epiphanes died and civil war erupted. Judas Maccabeus, who had succeeded his father Mattathias, extended his control over much of Palestine, including parts of Jerusalem. Three years to the day after its desecration the temple was cleansed, and the Syrians made peace with the Jews.

E. The Maccabean Era (166–37 B.C.). Judas Maccabeus was not allowed peace for long, and he quickly appealed to the Romans for assistance against Syria. Judas fell in battle before help arrived, and he was succeeded by his brother, Jonathan. Due to Syria's weakness, Jonathan became the commander of Judea. Upon his death he was succeeded by another brother, Simon, who also appealed to Rome for help. The Romans made Simon the ruler of Judea, and his throne was made hereditary.

By this time the parties of the Pharisees and Sadducees had rivals. When Simon's son, John Hyrcanus, succeeded him, he joined first one and then another of the opposing sects. Soon there was civil war as his two grandsons, Hyrcanus and Aristobulus, struggled for the throne vacated by his death. The Romans preferred Hyrcanus and the Roman general Pompey took Jerusalem from Aristobulus.

The ensuing sieges, battles, murders, and massacres mark a period of turmoil in Jewish history. Though they had been presented with an opportunity to restore Israel to a position of great power and influence, they wasted it with inter-family strife.

F. The Roman Dominance (From 37 B.C. through the New Testament period). Pompey, Crassus, and Julius Caesar reigned as the first triumvirate over Rome, but Julius Caesar soon became the sole ruler. He restored Hyrcanus to the throne in Jerusalem and appointed Antipater, a citizen of Idumea, as procurator under Hyrcanus. Antipater's two sons, Phasaelus and Herod, became governors of Judea and Galilee. The following year Antipater was poisoned; three years later Julius Caesar was assassinated in Rome.

A new triumvirate—Octavian (Caesar's nephew), Mark Antony, and Lepidus—then ruled Rome. Antony was over Syria and the East. He favored Herod, and this friendship led to the rise to power of this Idumean family. Herod married Mariamne, granddaughter of Hyrcanus and became a part of the Maccabean family.

A new disturbance arose in the land about this time. Antigonus, son of Aristobulus, gained a temporary success by causing the ears of Hyrcanus, the reigning high priest, to be cut off so that he could not qualify for the office. In the following struggle Herod was pressed by Antigonus, and he had to flee to the fortress called Masada for safety. He then went to Rome, described the disorder to the Romans, and was appointed king. Antigonus was put to death. This ended forever the rule of the Maccabees or Hasmoneans.

When shortly thereafter Antony committed suicide in Egypt, Herod extended his power in Judea. He lived in dread that a descendant of the Maccabees would rise in power to take his throne. When Aristobulus, a brother of Mariamne, was made high priest, his popularity led Herod to have him drowned. When Mariamne became enraged, he had her executed. In the years that followed Herod became increasingly vindictive, and his bloody deeds provoked the Jews' wrath.

To quiet the Jews' hostility, he launched a program of public works. His chief undertaking was the rebuilding of the temple.

But Herod's problems, and those of the nation, were not ended. He was surrounded by a group of men who exploited his paranoia. His two sons, like their mother Mariamne, fell

Corinth at the Crossroads

Corinth rose from ashes to occupy a position of prominence at the trading crossroads of the ancient world. The original city was destroyed in 146 B.C. in a Greek revolt against the Roman empire. Rebuilt in the time of Julius Caesar (*ca.* 46 B.C.), Corinth soon regained its former position as a center of commerce. Within twenty-one years, this rapidly growing metropolis became the capital of the province of Achaia in Greece.

Corinth was one of the wealthiest and most influential cities of its time. Located on a narrow strip of land between mainland Greece and the Peloponnesus (the peninsula of southern Greece), Corinth had two main harbors, which gave the city access to the Aegean and Ionian seas. This strategic location allowed Corinth to control the traffic of the eastern and western seas along a principal trade route of the Roman Empire. Corinth was the fourth largest city of the empire (after Rome, Alexandria, and Antioch), and had a population of nearly half a million.

Corinth was also situated at a cultural crossroads. Residents migrated to this rapidly developing area from every corner of the Mediterranean world. Egyptians, Syrians, Orientals, and Jews who settled there brought a wide variety of cultural influences.

One might well call ancient Corinth a "sin city." While rather low moral values were held by the general Roman public, Corinth had a reputation for embracing the lowest of the low. Even prior to the time of the apostle Paul, "to live like a Corinthian" was a slang phrase denoting loose, immoral conduct.

Oddly, religion contributed to this atmosphere of moral corruption. Many of the fertility cults that existed in the city included acts of magic and sexual perversion as part of their "worship." Corinth's temple of Aphrodite, the goddess of love, at one time had one thousand priestess-prostitutes within its confines.

To this complex city came the Apostle Paul. Arriving around A.D. 52, Paul remained there for about a year and a half, ministering to one of the greatest churches of Jesus Christ. A city at the crossroads, both physically and spiritually, Corinth heard the gospel of Christ through Paul's ministry.

Corinth was rebuilt after earthquakes in 1858 and 1928. The Doric columns of one old temple of Apollo are one of the few reminders of Corinth's early days left above the ground. Corinth today has a population of about 20,000. It is still an important sea town, with exports of olive oil, silk, and currants.

victim to his wrath and were strangled. On one occasion a large number of Pharisees met the same fate. Other equally bloody deeds continued throughout his reign. Toward the end of his life, this fear-filled ruler ordered the massacre of the babes of Bethlehem when the rival King of the Jews, Jesus, was born.

THE NEW TESTAMENT PERIOD

Four chapters appearing later in this book will recount the biblical facts of New Testament history (*Jesus Christ, The Apostles, The Early Church,* and *Paul and His Journeys*). This section will examine the political history of the New Testament era.

The Romans remained the supreme rulers of Palestine throughout New Testament times. The family of Herod, along with appointed Roman procurators, ruled under Rome's authority.

The New Testament opens with Jesus' birth. Herod the Great was king, but his rule was nearing its end. The last years of his reign had been filled with plot and counterplot as members of his family vied for his power. Shortly before the birth of Christ, he had executed his two sons by Mariamne. Another son, Antipater, plotted against Herod and was executed only five days before Herod's death in 4 B.C. To the Romans Herod had been a trustworthy and able vassal king, but to the Jews he had been a self-seeking tyrant.

His sons succeeded him. Archelaus (4 B.C.–A.D. 6) ruled in Judea. The least-liked of Herod's sons, he was cruel and despotic. The Jews' complaints against him ultimately brought about his exile. Herod Antipas (4 B.C.–A.D. 39) was appointed tetrarch of Galilee and Perea. This proud, clever ruler (Luke 13:32) was less brutal than Archelaus, but he murdered John the Baptist who had denounced his marriage to Herodias. Favored by the Roman emperor Tiberius (A.D. 14–37), he was exiled in A.D. 39 by Caligula (A.D. 37–41).

Philip (4 B.C.–A.D. 34), a third son of Herod, was tetrarch of the regions of Iturea and Trachonitus (Luke 3:1). Philip appears to have been a relatively just and benevolent ruler. His capital was Caesarea Philippi (Matthew 16:13; Mark 8:27), and his coins were the first Jewish coins to bear a human image (that of Augustus or Tiberius). He died in A.D. 34, and his territory was eventually added to that of Herod Agrippa I.

After the exile of Archelaus, his tetrarchy (Judea, Samaria, and Idumea) was ruled by Roman procurators (A.D. 6–41). Cyrenius, the prefect of Syria, came to Judea in A.D. 6 to enroll the people for purposes of taxation. This act provoked the patriots of Judea, but they were calmed for a moment by the Jewish authorities. However, Judas the Galilean led the people in revolt against the Romans and the Herods. He was soon killed (Acts 5:37); it is possible that his followers became the party of the Zealots (Luke 6:15; Acts 1:13).

The procurators of Judea were directly responsible to Rome. Living in Caesarea, they came to Jerusalem only on special occasions, such as the annual feasts. Augustus gave his procurators short terms, but Tiberius left them in office longer so that the people would not be exploited so often by newcomers. Pilate was the fifth procurator and was also the best-known because of his crucifixion of Jesus. An inflexible and harsh ruler, he was brutal to the Jews. His unwarranted massacre of worshiping Samaritans and other executions brought about his downfall in A.D. 36.

Herod Agrippa I rose to prominence in A.D. 37–44 and stripped the procurators of their powers. As the heir of the Maccabean, or Hasmonean, family and because of his observance of the Law, he was popular with the Pharisees. This popularity was enhanced by his hostility to the Christians (Acts 12). He died suddenly in A.D. 44, and his kingdom reverted to rule by the procurators. Conditions worsened under the procurators until they precipitated the Jewish rebellion against Roman rule in A.D. 66–70.

Fadus (A.D. 44–46) made the mistake of reclaiming custody of the high priestly garments, which resulted in a brief uprising. The garments had been in Roman hands from A.D. 6–36 but had been in Jewish hands from A.D. 36 to the time of

Synagogue at Capernaum. This is one of the best-preserved examples of synagogue architecture in Palestine. The style of the columns proves that the Jewish architects copied Greek models when they rebuilt the synagogue in the second or third century A.D.

Fadus. Alexander (A.D. 46–48) crucified the two sons of Judas the Galilean, James and Simon, for rebellion. Cumanus (A.D. 48–52) ruled an even more tumultuous era. When a Roman soldier made an indecent gesture during Passover, riots erupted and several people were killed. On another occasion, when a soldier tore up a scroll of the Law, Cumanus was forced to execute him when a multitude of Jews came to Caesarea to object. Such incidents eventually brought about his exile.

Felix (A.D. 52–60) was openly hostile toward the Jews, and his actions eventually led to war. His drastic measures to curb the Zealots, a group of Jewish patriots who advocated war with the Romans, only increased their popularity among the people. The *Sicarii,* or Assassins, arose from their midst. These fanatical Jews assassinated many, including Jonathan the high priest. His rule by terror and assassination united the fanatics with the masses and ultimately led to his recall to Rome.

Festus (A.D. 60–62) inherited a situation that was beyond control. Festus tried to pacify the countryside, but the fervor of the religious and political fanatics grew. When Festus died in office, anarchy completely prevailed in Jerusalem. It was during this time that James, the brother of Jesus, was killed. Rival high priests arose, vying for authority; and their followers fought pitched battles in the streets. When Albinus (A.D. 62–64) arrived in Jerusalem, he deliberately aggravated the trouble to promote his own position, rather than attempting to restore order. He arrested many, but he released those who would pay a large enough bribe.

Josephus reports that his successor, Florus (A.D. 64–66), was so evil and violent that he made Albinus look like a public benefactor. Florus plundered entire towns. He permitted robbers who paid bribes to ply their trade at will. Thus, the Jewish nation fell into an intolerable state. From A.D. 68 to 70 they fought a heroic war that ended in tragic defeat in A.D. 70 when the city and the temple were overrun and destroyed.

THE LIFE OF JESUS CHRIST

The New Testament brings us to the climax of God's redemptive work, because it introduces us to the Messiah, Jesus Christ, and to the beginning of His church. The writings of Matthew, Mark, Luke, and John tell us about Jesus' ministry. These writers were either eyewitnesses of Jesus' life or they wrote down what eyewitnesses told them, but they do not provide a full biography of Jesus. Everything they recorded actually happened, but they concentrate on Jesus' ministry and leave gaps elsewhere in the story of His life.

Imagine someone writing a letter to a friend to introduce him to an important person. Would the writer be able to describe *everything* about that person's life? Of course not. He could only write about what he knew—and he probably would not try to tell all of that, either. The writer would concentrate on what he thinks his friend wants and needs to know.

The men who wrote the Gospels did the same thing. They aimed to explain the *person* and *work* of Jesus by recording what He did and said. And each writer presents a slightly different view of Jesus and what He did. The Gospel writers did not try to relate all the events of Jesus' boyhood, because that was not their reason for writing. They did not try to give us a daily diary of Jesus' life either. They stuck to what matters for salvation and discipleship.

In this section we will take our cue from the Gospel writers. We will simply sketch the major events of Jesus' life and summarize how He brought the history of redemption to its climax. For more information about His life, see chapter 6, "Jesus Christ."

Many people know about the birth and infancy of Jesus Christ. Every Christmas we hear the well-known carols about the Virgin Mary (the mother of Jesus), her trip to Bethlehem on the back of a donkey, and the birth of the baby Jesus Christ—true man and true God, who came to earth to save God's people. We hear the familiar story of how Jesus was born in Bethlehem, of the manger where He lay, and of the angels who announced His birth to the shepherds. We know the angels declared Jesus to be the long-promised Davidic king.

The wise men who brought gifts to the Christ child are mystery figures. We don't know which country (or countries) they came from, only that they were "from the East" (Matt. 2:1). They may well have come from the great eastern empires of Mesopotamia, Babylonia, or Persia—They studied the stars and realized that a new king was being born among the Jews, and so they came to the Jewish capital of Jerusalem to pay their respects. How surprised they were to learn that King Herod had no new children! Then they followed a clear prophecy from Micah 5:2 that led them to Bethlehem, where they found the baby Jesus.

The Bible does not say there were *three* wise men, but artists have usually painted three to show the three gifts that they brought—gold, frankincense, and myrrh (Matt. 2:11). Apparently the *magi* came to see Jesus several months after He was born, and some scholars think Jesus may have been as much as two years old when they came.

After Jesus was born, His parents dedicated Him at the Temple in Jerusalem (Luke 2:22-28). They began training Him to live "in favor with God and man" (Luke 2:52).

King Herod wanted to be certain that the people did not

rally around the infant king to start a rebellion, so he ordered his soldiers to kill all the boy babies in Bethlehem (Matt. 2:16). Jesus' family fled into Egypt to escape the evil decree. After Herod died, they returned to Palestine and settled in the town of Nazareth.

The Bible says nothing else about Jesus until He was twelve or thirteen years old. Then, to assume His proper role in the Jewish congregation, He had to make a special visit to Jerusalem and offer a sacrifice at the temple. While He was there, Jesus talked with religious leaders about the Jewish faith. He showed an extraordinary understanding of the true God, and His answers amazed them. Later, His parents started home and discovered that Jesus was missing. They found Him at the temple, still talking with the Jewish experts.

Again, the Bible falls silent until it introduces us to the events that began Jesus' ministry when He was about thirty years old. First we see John the Baptist coming out of the wilderness and preaching in cities along the Jordan River, urging the people to prepare for their Messiah (Luke 3:3-9). John had been born into a godly family, and he grew up to love and serve God faithfully. God spoke through John, and crowds of people clamored to hear his preaching. He told them to return to God and begin obeying Him. When he saw Jesus he cried that this man was the ". . . Lamb of God, which taketh away the sin of the world" (John 1:29). John baptized Jesus; and as Jesus came up from the water, God sent the Holy Spirit in the form of a dove that settled upon Jesus.

The Holy Spirit led Jesus into the wilderness, where He went without food for forty days. While He was in this weakened condition, the Devil came and tried to tempt Him in various ways. Jesus refused and sent the Devil away. Then angels came to feed Jesus and comfort Him.

At first, Jesus was a popular man. In the area around the Sea of Galilee, He attended a wedding feast and changed water into wine to serve the guests. This is the first of His miracles that the Bible mentions. It demonstrated that He truly was God, just as His later miracles did. From Galilee, He went to Jerusalem and drove a group of religious hucksters out of the temple. For the first time, publicly He asserted His authority over the religious life of His people. This turned many of the other religious leaders against Him.

One of those leaders, Nicodemus, saw that Jesus was teaching the truth about God. He came to Jesus one night and asked how He could get into the kingdom of God, which is the realm of redemption and salvation. Jesus told Nicodemus that he must "be born again" (John 3:3); in other words, he had to become a new person. From this conversation between Jesus and Nicodemus, we learn that a Christian is a person who has been "born again."

When John the Baptist began preaching and drawing great crowds in Judea, Jesus went back to the district of Galilee. There He performed many miracles and was surrounded by large crowds. Unfortunately, the crowds were more interested in the miracles than in Jesus' teachings.

Golden gate. Located in the eastern wall of the temple area, this fifth-century A.D. structure is thought to have been built on the place where Christ made His triumphal entry into Jerusalem (cf. Matt. 21:8-11). The Turkish governor of Jerusalem blocked the gate in 1530.

Yet Jesus kept on teaching. He entered private homes, sat at public feasts, and worshiped with other Jews at their synagogues. He denounced the religious leaders of His day because their faith was a sham. He didn't reject their formal religion; on the contrary, Jesus respected the temple and temple worship (cf. Matt. 5:17-18). But the Pharisees and other leaders failed to see that He was the Messiah, and they didn't care about being saved from sin. Furthermore, they were not satisfied with what God had revealed to them in the Old Testament, but kept adding to it and revising it. They believed their worked-over version of the Scriptures gave them the only true religion. Jesus called them back to God's original words. He was very careful about the way He quoted Scripture, and He prodded his followers to understand it better. He taught that even a basic knowledge of Scripture should show a person God's will for salvation through faith in himself.

Near Galilee, Jesus performed His most amazing miracle yet. He took seven loaves of bread and two fish, blessed them, and broke them into enough pieces to feed four thousand people! But this did not draw more people to faith in Jesus; in fact, they turned away because they couldn't figure out why and how He wanted them to "eat" His body and "drink" His blood (John 6:52-66).

The twelve disciples stayed true to Jesus, and He began to focus His efforts on training them. He increasingly taught them about His coming death and resurrection, explaining that they also could expect to suffer death if they kept on following Him.

This brings us to the end of Jesus Christ's life on earth. Judas Iscariot, one of Jesus' twelve disciples, betrayed Him to the hostile leaders of Jerusalem, and they nailed Him to a wooden cross to die among common criminals. But He rose from the grave and appeared to many of His followers, just as He had promised, and gave final instructions to His closest disciples. As they watched Him ascend into heaven, an angel appeared and said they would see Him return in the same way. In other words, He would come back visibly and in His physical body.

THE MINISTRY OF THE APOSTLES

Bible history ends in the Book of Acts, which describes the ministry of the early church. In Acts we see how the message concerning Jesus—the message of redemption—spread from Jerusalem to Rome, the center of the Western world. The Book of Acts shows the expansion of the church (a) in Jerusalem, (b) from Jerusalem into Judea, Samaria, and the surrounding area, and (c) from Antioch to Rome.

A. In Jerusalem. The early experiences of Jesus' disciples in Jerusalem reveal a great deal about the early church. The Book of Acts shows how earnestly these Christians spread the news about Jesus.

The book opens on a hillside near Jerusalem, where Jesus was about to ascend into heaven. He told His disciples, ". . . after that the Holy Ghost is come upon you: and ye shall be witnesses unto me both in Jerusalem, and in all Judea, and in Samaria, and unto the uttermost part of the earth" (Acts 1:8). That was Jesus' plan to evangelize the world.

A few days later the disciples replaced Judas, who had killed himself after he betrayed Jesus. They chose Matthias to round out the group of twelve.

Then the risen Christ gave the church His Holy Spirit, who enabled the Christians to fulfill their worldwide task (Acts 1:8).

Peter spoke for the church on the Day of Pentecost; he unfolded the importance of Christ as the Lord of salvation (Acts 2:14-40). The Holy Spirit empowered the church to perform signs and wonders that confirmed the truthfulness of this message (Acts 2:43). Especially significant was the apostles' cure of a beggar at the door to the temple (Acts 3:1-10), which brought the apostles into conflict with the Jewish authorities.

The church maintained a close fellowship among its members. They shared meals in their homes; they also worshiped together and shared their wealth (Acts 2:44-46; 5:32-34). One couple named Ananias and Sapphira tried to deceive the church; having sold their property, they claimed to be giving *all* of the proceeds to the Lord, but they gave only a portion. God struck them dead for lying (Acts 5:1-11).

As the church continued to grow, government authorities began to persecute Christians openly. When Peter and some of the apostles were imprisoned, an angel released them, but they were called back before the authorities who ordered them to stop preaching about Jesus (Acts 5:17-29). But the Christians refused to stop preaching, even though the Jewish religious leaders beat them and threw them into prison several times.

The church grew so rapidly that the apostles needed help in some of the practical matters of church administration, notably their ministry to widows. They ordained seven deacons for this task. One of the seven, Stephen, began to preach in the streets. Eventually the religious authorities stoned him to death (Acts 7:54-60).

B. From Jerusalem into All Judea. The second stage of the church's growth opened with a violent persecution of the church in Jerusalem. Almost all the believers fled from the city (Acts 8:1). Wherever the Christians went they witnessed, and the Holy Spirit used their testimony to win other people to Christ (Acts 8:3ff.). For example, another of the apostles' seven helpers named Philip talked to an Ethiopian diplomat, who became a Christian and took the good news to his homeland (Acts 8:26-39).

At this point the Bible describes the conversion of Saul of Tarsus. Before his conversion Saul persecuted the church. He obtained letters from the Jewish leaders in Jerusalem, authorizing him to proceed to Damascus to make sure that the Christians there were imprisoned and put to death. On his way, Christ struck him down and challenged him. Saul surrendered and thus began a new life in which he was to use his Roman name, Paul, in place of his Jewish name, Saul. God led him blind to Damascus, where God sent a Christian man named Ananias to him. Through Ananias, Paul's sight was

The street called Straight. A small arch is all that remains of the old city gate that stood in Damascus in Paul's day. The arch leads to "the street called Straight," where Paul stayed just after his conversion (Acts 9:11).

restored and he was filled with the Holy Spirit. Paul began to preach about Jesus in the Jewish synagogue, and the Jewish leaders drove him out of Damascus. Some time later (cf. Gal. 1:17–2:2) he went to Jerusalem, where he established a working relationship with the apostles.

We should also notice the ministry of Peter, which was especially marked with miracles. In Lydda he healed a man named Aeneas (Acts 9:32-35). In Joppa, God used him to raise Tabitha from the dead (Acts 9:36-42). Finally, God gave him a vision that summoned him to Caesarea, where he introduced the gospel to the Gentiles (Acts 10:9-48).

Peter was the foremost leader of the apostles and his ministry rallied the enthusiasm of the early church. An *apostle* was a person whom Christ had chosen for special training in ministry (cf. Gal. 1:12). The apostles laid the foundation of the church by preaching the gospel of Christ (cf. Eph. 2:20; 1 Cor. 3:10-11; Jude 3:20. *See also* chapter 7, "The Apostles"). God used Peter to open the door of salvation to the Gentiles.

At this point the record of Bible history turns briefly to the expansion of the gospel among the Gentiles in Antioch (Acts 11:19-30). Then we read of James' martyrdom in Jerusalem, and how Peter was miraculously delivered from prison (Acts 12:1-19).

C. From Antioch to Rome. The rest of the Book of Acts describes the expansion of the church through the ministry of the apostle Paul. Barnabas brought Paul to Antioch (Acts 11:19-26). There the Holy Spirit called Barnabas and Paul to be missionaries, and the church ordained them for this task (Acts 13:1-3).

The map entitled "Paul's First Missionary Journey" traces the route of their first church-planting campaign. *(See also* chapter 9, "Paul and His Journeys.")* Generally, Paul and Barnabas would begin by preaching in a local Jewish synagogue. Thus the early church consisted primarily of converts from among Jews and "God-fearers" (Gentiles who worshiped with the Jews). This first journey saw a dramatic confrontation with evil when God used Paul to defeat the sorcerer Elymas (Acts 13:6-12). Young John Mark accompanied Paul and Barnabas, but he decided to turn back at Perga; this must have been very disappointing to Paul (cf. Acts 15:38).

Read the sermon Paul delivered in the synagogue at Antioch of Pisidia (Acts 13:16-41). In it he gives a brief summary of the history of redemption, emphasizing its fulfillment in Jesus Christ. Paul declared that believing in Christ is the only way to be free from sin and death (vv. 38-39).

At Lystra, hostile Jews stirred up crowds so that Paul was stoned and left for dead (Acts 14:8-19). The journey ended with Paul and Barnabas returning to Antioch, where they reported all that God had done through them and how the faith had spread to the Gentiles (Acts 14:26-29).

Later a serious disagreement arose in the church. Some Christians argued that the gentile converts had to follow the

Old Testament laws, particularly the law of circumcision. Finally, the issue went before an assembly of church leaders from Antioch and Jerusalem. God directed this council (which met in Jerusalem) to declare that Gentiles did not have to keep the Law to be saved. But they instructed the new converts that they should abstain from eating things sacrificed to idols, blood, and strangled animals (Acts 15:1-29), so as not to offend the Jewish converts. The council sent a letter to Antioch where the church read it and accepted it as God's will.

Paul soon decided to return to all the churches he and Barnabas had established on the first missionary journey. And so the second missionary journey began (Acts 15:40-41). Especially note the vision God gave Paul in Troas, which summoned them to Macedonia (Acts 16:9-10). In Macedonia, they led "Godfearers" (Gentiles who believed in God) and Jews into the faith.

One day the missionaries encountered a demon-possessed slave girl. Her owners profited from her ability to tell for-

Corinth. The ruins of the temple of Apollo give mute testimony to the pagan worship of Corinth, where Paul directed two of his earliest epistles. Located on the narrow isthmus of Achaia, Corinth had two harbors—one on the Aegean and one on the Adriatic Sea. Thus it was an important crossroads of the ancient world.

tunes. Paul cast the demons out of the girl and she lost her powers, so her owners arrested the missionaries (Acts 16:19-24). While in prison, Paul and his friends converted the jailer. They were released in the morning and went to Thessalonica, where many people were converted under their ministry. Next they went to Berea, where they also had great success (Acts 17:10-12). In Athens, Paul preached a remarkable sermon to the Greek philosophers on Mars Hill.

The next stop was Corinth, where Paul and his friends stayed a year and a half. From there they journeyed back to Antioch via Jerusalem (Acts 18:18-22). All this time, Paul and his companions continued to preach in the synagogues, and faced opposition from some Jews who rejected the gospel (Acts 18:12-17).

The third missionary journey covered many of the same cities Paul had visited on the second journey. He also made a quick visit to the churches in Galatia and Phrygia (Acts 18:23).

In Ephesus he baptized twelve of John the Baptist's disciples who had accepted Christ and they received the Holy Spirit (Acts 19:1-6). He preached in the Ephesian school of Tyrannus for nearly two years (Acts 19:9-10).

From Ephesus he went to Macedonia and finally back to Philippi. After a brief stay in Philippi he journeyed to Troas, where a young man named Eutychus fell asleep while listening to one of Paul's sermons and plummeted from a third-story window to his death. God worked through Paul to bring Eutychus back to life (Acts 20:7-12). From there, the missionaries went by way of Miletus to Caesarea where the prophet Agabus predicted that danger awaited Paul in Jerusalem.

In Jerusalem, Paul met trouble and imprisonment. The Bible records a speech he made there in defense of his Christian faith (Acts 22:1-21). Eventually the religious authorities succeeded in sending him to Rome for trial. On the way to Rome, the ship carrying him wrecked on the island of Malta ("Melita"). There a poisonous snake bit Paul, but he was not harmed (Acts 28:3-6). Paul then cured the sick father of Publius, the political leader of the island (Acts 28:7-8). After three months on Malta, Paul and his guards sailed for Rome.

The Book of Acts ends with Paul's activities in Rome. We read that he preached to the leading Jews there (Acts 28:17-20). He lived for two years in a rented house, continuing to preach to the people who visited him (Acts 28:30-31). For a more detailed description of Paul's life, see chapter 9, "Paul and His Journeys."

This closes the Bible's history of redemption. The gospel had been effectively planted in gentile soil, and most of the New Testament Epistles had been written. The church was in the process of separating itself from the Jewish synagogue and becoming a distinct organization.

2
NEW TESTAMENT CHRONOLOGY

Scripture tells how God revealed Himself at specific points in time. To help grasp the relation of these divine revelations to other historical events, we need to know the dates of the biblical events themselves.

The word *chronology* comes from the classical Greek word *chronos,* which signifies time viewed as a flowing stream—a stream that cannot be stopped, but can be measured. *Chronology* is simply the dating of historical events within the "stream" of time. The Bible devotes quite a lot of space to matters of chronology.

For instance, the prophets dated their writings to show the background of their message. Their chronological notes help us understand why God said what He said, and why He did what He did at each particular time.

Jewish people followed their calendar with great care. Ancient Israel had a lunar calendar that pegged religious festivals to certain seasons of the year. The Israelites harvested barley in the spring during Abib, the first month of the religious year (Exod. 23:15). After the Exile, they called this month Nisan. They celebrated the Feast of Weeks during the month of Sivan, which began the summer harvest of wheat (Exod. 34:22). Their Feast of the Ingathering (or Feast of Booths) coincided with their general harvest in the autumn month of Ethanim, later called Tishri (Exod. 34:22). Generally their months were 30 days long. But since each month was counted from a new-moon day, the calendar sometimes called for a 29-day month. The lunar calendar was 11 days shorter than the solar year and yet had to match the seasons, so the Israelites sometimes had to add a thirteenth month to the year. This gave them some leap-year days. Their pattern of inserting leap-year days repeated itself in a 19-year cycle.

When we come to the New Testament, we find that a number of important chronological details are included. But, like the Old Testament, the New Testament does not give us dates in the same way that we get them from our calendar.

THE LIFE OF JESUS

Because the Jewish people—as is true of all ancient peoples—did not operate by the calendar that is used today, we must exercise great care in dating the events of Jesus' life. Fortunately, the New Testament and various secular sources can be used in finding the approximate dates for these events.

A. Birth. Herod the Great was king in Judea when Jesus was born (Matt. 2:1). Josephus writes in his *Antiquities* that there was an eclipse of the moon just before the death of Herod (Bk. XVII, Chap. xiii, Sect. 2). This might refer to any of three eclipses in 5 and 4 B.C.; the most likely choice is March 12, 4 B.C. Furthermore, this Jewish historian states that the king died just before Passover (Bk. XVII, Chap. vi, Sect. 4) and Passover occurred on April 11 in 4 B.C. So we must conclude that Herod died in the early part of April that year.

Wise men from the East came to worship God's Messiah. But when they did not report back to him, Herod ordered his soldiers to kill all babies in Bethlehem, two years and under (Matt. 2:16). This suggests that Jesus was born in 6 or 5 B.C. and He was between one and two years old when Herod died. He was probably born in 5 B.C., and was taken to Egypt sometime in 4 B.C.

We don't know the exact month and day when Jesus was born. The date December 25 is not very likely. The church in Rome chose that day to celebrate His birth in the second or third century in order to obscure a thoroughly pagan holiday that was traditionally celebrated on that day. Earlier the Eastern Orthodox church chose to honor Christ's birth on January 6, Epiphany. But why set the date in the winter? The shepherds would have been least likely to tend their flocks on the hillsides at that time. More likely, Jesus was born in the fall or spring.

Many scholars think the star of Bethlehem (Matt. 2:2) was some astronomical event. They say that perhaps it was a time when the planets Saturn and Jupiter appeared to cross paths in the sky; that happened in 7 or 6 B.C. Others note that Chinese records tell of a very bright star or comet in 5 and 4 B.C. But there are great problems with either theory. The Scriptures say that the star guided the wise men on their journey and even marked out the house, so that they would not be mistaken (Matt. 2:9-10). While the star did spark the interest of these wise men, it does not help us determine when Jesus was born.

B. Beginning of Ministry. The New Testament tells us much concerning Jesus' service in public; but again we must correlate these statements with outside sources to find the dates.

John the Baptist crossed the careers of several historical figures in Judea and the Roman Empire (Luke 3:1). For our purposes, the most important was Tiberius Caesar, who, Luke tells us, had been in office 4 years at the beginning of John's ministry. Josephus indicates that Tiberius became emperor at the death of Augustus in A.D. 14 (*Antiquities* Bk. XVIII, Chap. ii, Sect. 2). His fifteenth year would therefore have been A.D. 28 or 29, depending on whether he used an accession or a non-accession scheme of dating. John and Jesus began their ministry at about the same time. Let us assume that Jesus had a ministry of three and a half years and was about 30 years of age, as Luke 3:23 says, when He began to serve. At once a problem emerges: Josephus' date for Tiberius requires us to place the death of Jesus in about A.D. 31 or 32, and to move His birth date to 3 or 2 B.C., which as we saw is too late.

However, the problem is not insuperable. We know that Tiberius ruled with Augustus Caesar for two or three years before Augustus died. This means he began his official duties in about A.D. 11 or 12, and on this reckoning the fifteenth year of his rulership came in A.D. 26 or 27. The date of A.D. 26 is probably the best choice for the beginning of John's and Jesus' ministry, because it squares with the 5-6 B.C. birth date of Jesus.

The Bible says that Jesus was about 30 years of age when He

THE INTERTESTAMENTAL PERIOD

PALESTINE/JUDEA	Date B.C.	PERSIA
Ezra returns to Jerusalem	458	
Nehemiah returns to Jerusalem	444	
Malachi's ministry begins	430	
		GREECE
	332	Alexander takes Jerusalem from Persia
	323	Death of Alexander
		EGYPT
	323	Ptolemy Sater begins rule
Simon made high priest	300	
Eleazar made high priest	291	
	285	Ptolemy Philadelphus begins rule
Onias II made high priest	250	
	247	Ptolemy Euergetes begins rule
	222	Ptolemy Philopater begins rule
	204	Ptolemy Epiphanes begins rule
		SYRIA
	198	Antiochus the Great annexes Palestine
	187	Seleucis IV begins rule
Onias III made high priest	180	
	175	Antiochus IV Epiphanes begins rule
Jason buys the high priesthood	170	
Oppression of the Jews is intensified	168	
The Temple is desecrated	167	
The Maccabees begin their revolt against Syrian rule		
Judas Maccabeus assumes leadership of the revolt	166	
	164	Antiochus V Eupator begins rule
	162	Demetrius I Soter begins rule

began His ministry, right after His baptism (Luke 3:1-2, 21-23). But what did *about* 30 years" signify? The priests began their service at 30 years of age, but Jesus was not a Levitical priest and was not bound to this rule. On the other hand, it was a respectable age. From a Jewish point of view, a man of 30 was not too young to be in a position of spiritual authority, yet not too old to carry on a vigorous ministry. We should accept that Jesus began his ministry very near the age of 30.

Herod's reconstruction of the temple confirms our date for

Death of Judas Maccabeus	161	
Jonathan Maccabeus succeeds Judas		
Jonathan is murdered	144	
Simon Maccabeus succeeds Jonathan		
	143	Antiochus VII Sidetos begins rule
Simon is murdered	135	
John Hyrcanus succeeds Simon		
	130	The Syrians are expelled
Aristobulus I succeeds John Hyrcanus	104	
Alexander Janneus succeeds Aristobulus I	103	
Death of Alexander Janneus	78	
Alexandra, the wife of Alexander Janneus, succeeds	76	
Death of Alexandra	69	
Hyrcanus II succeeds Alexandra		
Aristobulus II in conflict with Hyrcanus II (68–40 B.C.)	68	
		ROME
Judea falls to Rome	63	Pompey establishes Roman protectorate
	59	The First Triumverate: Pompey, Caesar, Crassus
	54	Crassus plunders the temple
	48	Death of Pompey
		Julius Caesar begins rule
Antipater appointed governor of Galilee	47	
	44	Julius Caesar assassinated
Death of Antipater	37	
Herod becomes king of Judea		
	33	War breaks out between Octavian and Antony
	31	Suicide of Antony and Cleopatra
Herod murders Mariamne	29	
	27	Octavian becomes Caesar Augustus
Herod begins to rebuild the Temple	19	
Birth of John the Baptist	6	
Birth of Jesus Christ	5	

Figure 1

the beginning of Jesus' ministry. Roman history shows that Herod became king of Judea in 37 B.C. Josephus says that the Jews began to refurbish the second temple in the eighteenth year of Herod's reign, or in 19 B.C. (37 B.C. minus 18). When Jesus was in Jerusalem for the Passover, people told Him that the reconstruction was in its forty-sixth year (John 2:13, 20). This would place Jesus' first visit in A.D. 27. We assume that Jesus had already begun his ministry when he visited Jerusalem; so he would have begun his work sometime in the fall of A.D. 26.

C. Length of Ministry. Many regular events of Jewish life appear in Jesus' ministry. The most prominent of these was the feast of the Passover. The Gospel of John mentions three Passovers during Jesus' ministry (John 2:13; 6:4; 12:1). A. T. Robertson's *Harmony of the Gospels* shows that John 5:1 also refers to a Passover feast. Since Jesus began His ministry before the first of the four Passovers, the length of His ministry was three-and-one-half years, beginning sometime in the fall of A.D. 26 and concluding in the spring Passover season of A.D. 30.

Can we be more precise about the date of Jesus' death? Perhaps. The Jewish calendar shows that the Passover came on April 7, A.D. 30. Tradition says that Jesus was crucified on Friday; that would put the Passover on Thursday evening— Nisan 14 on the Jewish calendar. Some scholars, however, think that the crucifixion took place on Thursday, or even Wednesday.

And there is another problem: Did Jesus really eat a Passover meal, or just some *kind* of significant meal? It is inconceivable that Jesus would have sent His disciples to

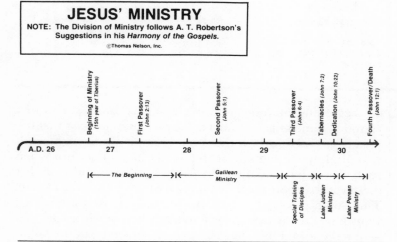

Figure 3

prepare the Passover (Luke 22:8, 13), without expecting them to offer the proper sacrifice in the temple and set an actual Passover table. Any other feast at that time of the year would have been unthinkable.

And how did the Jewish people calculate the new moon, which sets the date of the Passover meal? (They celebrated Passover 14 days after the new moon of the first month of Nisan.) If they reckoned the day of the new moon by a calculation of astronomy, they would have celebrated Passover on April 7, A.D. 30. But if they used a visual observation of the moon to determine the date of Passover, they could have made some error. But A. T. Robertson argues for the traditional date of Passover—April 7, A.D. 30—because it allows us to harmonize the narratives of the Synoptics (Matthew, Mark, and Luke) with the Gospel of John. Figure 14 shows how these dates plot the various phases of Jesus' ministry.

THE MINISTRY OF PAUL

The chronology of the life of Paul cannot be pinpointed as accurately as Jesus', but a good approximation can be made. References in the Book of Acts and his epistles, especially Galatians, give much helpful information. Saul was born in Tarsus, probably during the latter years of Herod or in the earlier years of his son, Archelaus. Through his father, a strict Jew of the tribe of Benjamin, he received the great privilege of Roman citizenship. According to custom, he was taught a trade, that of tentmaking, and was well educated at the feet of Gamaliel.

A dramatic turnabout in the life of Saul—later known as Paul—occurred around A.D. 36 as he journeyed to Damascus in his persecution of the Christians. The voice of Jesus spoke to him out of a blinding light from heaven, and he was struck blind. In the events which followed he received his sight again, was "filled with the Holy Ghost," was baptized, and confessed Jesus as the Son of God (Acts 9:17-20). The next three years

NEW TESTAMENT CHRONOLOGY

BIBLICAL EVENTS	Date	POLITICAL EVENTS
	B.C.	
Birth of John the Baptist	6	
Birth of Jesus Christ	5	
	4	Death of Herod
		Reign of Archelaus, Herod Antipas, and Herod Philip
	A.D.	
	7	Annas appointed high priest
Visit of Jesus to the Temple	8	
	14	Death of Augustus
		Ascension of Tiberius Caesar
	17	Caiaphas appointed high priest
John the Baptist begins his preaching ministry	27	Herod Antipas meets Herodias in Italy
Baptism of Jesus		
Jesus' ministry begins		
John the Baptist imprisoned	28	Herod Antipas marries Herodias
John the Baptist beheaded	29	
Crucifixion of Jesus	30	
Martyrdom of Stephen	36	
Conversion of Saul		
Dispersion of the Christians		
	37	Death of Tiberius
		Ascension of Caligula
Peter's visit to the churches	39	
Saul completes three-year stay in Arabia	40	
Saul visits Jerusalem		
Conversion of Cornelius	41	Death of Caligula
		Ascension of Claudius
Spread of the gospel to Antioch	42	
	43	Herod Agrippa I becomes king
Martyrdom of James, the son of Zebedee	44	Death of Herod Agrippa I
Saul brought to Antioch by Barnabas	46	
Saul and Barnabas bring Antioch's contributions to the Jerusalem church	47	
Paul and Barnabas' First Missionary Journey	48–49	
The Jerusalem Council	50	
The Gospel of Mark written		
The Second Missionary Journey	51–53	

were spent in Arabia. From there he returned to Damascus. He made his first journey to Jerusalem as a Christian in A.D. 40. The next years of his life were spent in Syria and Cilicia, much of it in his home area of Tarsus (Gal. 1:21).

Barnabas, an early Christian leader, was sent by the believers in Jerusalem to view the situation in Antioch. There a large contingent of Gentiles was responding to the gospel.

First and Second Thessalonians written		
	52	Felix made procurator of Judea
Paul's fourth visit to Jerusalem	54	Death of Claudius
Paul begins Third Missionary Journey		Ascension of Nero
Paul arrives at Ephesus		
The Epistles of First and Second Corinthians written	54–57	
Paul goes to Corinth	57	
The letter to the Romans written		
The Epistle to the Galatians written		
Paul is arrested	58	
The Gospel of Luke written	58–63	
Paul is sent to Rome	60	Festus succeeds Felix
Paul reaches Rome	61	
The writing of the epistles to Philemon, the Colossians, Ephesians and Philippians.	62	Albinus succeeds Festus
Paul released from prison in Rome	63	
The Acts of the Apostles written		
Paul visits Philippi (and Asia Minor?)		
Paul's Journey to Spain (?)	64	Florus succeeds Albinus
First Peter written		
Paul's return to Asia Minor	66	
Second Peter written		
Paul's Journey to Macedonia	67	
First Timothy written		
Paul's visit to Crete		
The Epistle to Titus written		
Paul's second imprisonment	68	Death of Nero
Second Timothy written		
Paul's martyrdom		
The Epistle to the Hebrews written		
	70	Destruction of Jerusalem and the Temple by the Romans
		Dispersion of the Jews throughout the Roman Empire
The Gospel of Matthew written	75	
First John written	85–90	
The Gospel of John written	90–100	
The Book of Revelation written	96	
Second John written		
Third John written	97	

Figure 2

Barnabas, who probably was familiar with Paul's call to minister to Gentiles, sought him out and brought him from Tarsus to Antioch in A.D. 46. About a year later the church at Antioch sent a gift to Jerusalem by the hand of Paul and Barnabas. Thus he made his second journey to Jerusalem as a Christian.

After returning to Antioch Paul and Barnabas set out on a

The Alexandrian Library

Alexander the Great reached Egypt in November 332 B.C. On January 20, 331 B.C., Alexander himself drew in the sands an outline for a new city to be the center of his navy and Greek culture—Alexandria. It would incorporate the old Egyptian town of Ratotis and Neopolis (new city) in its walls. Dinocrates, the architect of Rhodes, was left in charge of the building project.

Alexandria became the site of three wonders of the ancient world: the lighthouse of Pharos (an island connected to the mainland with a causeway); the Soma, which housed Alexander's golden coffin; and the most famous library in the ancient world, the Alexandrian Library.

The idea for a library in Alexandria seems to have originated with Ptolemy I Soter (d. 283 B.C.), who began collecting manuscripts for it. The actual library building was probably erected by Ptolemy II Philadelphus (285–246 B.C.). Most of Alexandria's archeological evidence dating from this period is lost, although scholars accompanying Napoleon Bonaparte recorded in 1799 that the city's ruins (which had served for centuries as a quarry for new building) still constituted a considerably large complex. Modern Alexandria was built on the same site and obliterated most of the ruins, including the library.

The library was a part of the *Mouseion* ("House of the Muses," or house of arts and sciences), which was patterned on Aristotle's Lyceum in Athens. The Mouseion was a complex of buildings connected by long colonnades. In these colonnades were study rooms, lecture halls, and administrative offices where scholars could teach and do research. Among the scholars who used the library were the mathematicians Euclid and Apollonios of Perga, the geographer Eratosthenis (who first said the world was round), the astronomer Aristarchos of Samos, and the medical researchers Ersistratos and Eudemos.

The library building had two parts: "the library within the palace" (the *Brucheion*) and the smaller "library outside the palace" (the *Serepheum*). By 250 B.C., the Brucheion contained 400,000 "mixed volumes" (longer scrolls containing more than one work) and 90,000 single volumes; the Serepheum contained 42,800 volumes. The Serepheum served the ordinary students and citizens.

Ptolemy II also issued orders that his soldiers should seize any books found on ships unloading in Alexandria. These books were then copied and a copy was returned to the owners. Books received in this manner were labelled "from the ships." The ancient writer Galen recounted how Ptolemy III Euergetes tricked the Athenians into lending him their official copies of the tragedies—the copies which the actors used in their performances—and then forfeited the security deposit of fifteen talents when he kept the original as well as the copy he had made.

The books were first housed in warehouses until they could be processed. Library workers took great care in labelling the copies, to show the source of each manuscript. The books might be labelled by the geographical origin, by the name of the corrector or editor of the copy, or by the name of the owner. Callimachus, who may have been one of the chief librarians, is said to have compiled a document called the *Pinakes* for library users. The *Pinakes* was subtitled, "Tables of Those Who Were Outstanding in Every Phase of Culture, and Their Writings."

The decline of the Mouseion and library seems to have begun about 100 B.C., amid wars and civil unrest. It seems that the Brucheion was accidently burned by Julius Caesar in the Alexandria War in 48 B.C. Although much irreplaceable material was lost when the Brucheion was destroyed, Mark Antony compensated for the loss by giving Cleopatra 200,000 manuscripts from the library at Pergamum. From this time, the Serepheum took the place of the Brucheion as the royal library.

The library declined further after the beginning of the Christian Era. It was burned again by the Roman emperor Aurelian in A.D. 273 as he reconquered Egypt. Whatever was left of the library was finally destroyed by the Moslem conqueror Omar in A.D. 645.

missionary journey that took them to Cyprus, Perga, Antioch in Pisidia, Iconium, Lystra, and Derbe (Acts 13–14). This was around A.D. 48–49. This first missionary journey was the most fruitful missionary effort the church had made to this time.

The growth of the gentile church in Antioch and the response of Gentiles in other places raised the question of the relationship of the Gentiles to the Law. Visitors from Jerusalem were causing turmoil in the church at Antioch, and Paul and Barnabas were dispatched to Jerusalem to deal with the problem. This council took place around A.D. 50.

Upon their return to Antioch, Paul and Barnabas planned another journey. When they could not agree about taking John Mark with them, they decided to separate. Paul chose Silas for his companion and left on his second missionary journey. This journey through Galatia, Macedonia, and Achaia occupied the years A.D. 51–53. About eighteen months were spent in Corinth, where he wrote the two epistles to the church at Thessalonica.

When he left Corinth he took Priscilla and Aquila, whom he left at Ephesus. From there he journeyed to Jerusalem—his

Herod's Temple. Dr. Conrad Shick has constructed this scale model of the temple in Jerusalem as it might have looked after Herod's massive restoration program (19 B.C.–A.D. 63). The model reflects information from early Jewish writers and archaeological finds in the temple area.

fourth visit—in A.D. 54. After hurried visits to Jerusalem and Antioch, he launched his third missionary journey. He appears to have spent nearly three years in Ephesus (A.D. 54–57). Largely successful, still his experience here was full of opposition and peril. The problems in Corinth added to his burdens, and he wrote his letters to the Corinthians from here.

Leaving Ephesus, he journeyed to Corinth for a three-month stay. He may have written the Book of Galatians, and did write the Epistle to the Romans, at this time. Shortly thereafter, he made his fifth visit to Jerusalem.

Quickly arrested in Jerusalem, he was sent to Caesarea where he was imprisoned for two years (A.D. 58–60). With no resolution of the charges in view, he appealed his case to Caesar and was sent to Rome. Living in custody—part of the time in his own rented lodging (Acts 28:30)—he wrote the epistles of Ephesians, Colossians, Philippians, and Philemon. After the two years of imprisonment in Rome (A.D. 61–63) mentioned in Acts 28:30, we have no factual record of where he went and what he did. Tradition says that he preached the gospel to the "extremities of the west," supposedly Spain. He is believed to have visited Crete (Titus 1:5), Ephesus (1 Tim. 1:3), and Nicopolis (Titus 3:12) in Macedonia from whence he wrote to Titus.

The First Epistle of Clement, written shortly before A.D. 200, states that he was taken prisoner once again around A.D. 67 in Macedonia and was sent to Rome for a second imprisonment. It is believed that he wrote his final epistle—Second Timothy—there and that he died a martyr at Nero's command in the spring or summer of A.D. 68.

Keys to dating Paul's ministry include the succession of Felix by Festus (Acts 24:27; 25:1), which took place in approximately A.D. 60, and the term of office of Gallio in Achaia around A.D. 56. Most of his ministry took place during the relative peace of the reign of Claudius (A.D. 41–54). Some would place his death earlier than A.D. 68. Some scholars do not believe that he was released from the first Roman imprisonment and that he was put to death at the time that the Book of Acts closes, around A.D. 64.

3

THE GREEKS AND HELLENISM

Ancient Greeks called their land Hellas and they called themselves Hellenes. The most influential of the Greek city-states was Athens, which provided the major inspiration for the achievements of the Greek Empire that was briefly to stretch across territories nearly as large as the United States of America.

When we speak of *"Hellenic* culture," we mean the Greek cultural achievements that reached their highest point in Athens in the fifth century B.C. "Hellenic culture" signifies the arts, commerce, and thought of the Greek mainland as it was influenced by Athens. *"Hellenistic* culture" is the subsequent development of Greek culture among other eastern Mediterranean peoples who reflected the culture begun in Athens. This Greek way of life was carried as far as India by the armies of Alexander the Great. It remained long enough in Egypt, Palestine, Asia Minor, and Persia to influence their religion, government, language, and art.

EARLY GREEK HISTORY

War and political intrigue checkered the early history of Greece. The Greeks' ability to overcome these problems indicated their strong character and hopeful vision of the future.

A. Roots of Greek Culture. The Greek islands and the Greek mainland were inhabited by people called the Aegeans by about 3000 B.C. The Minoans inhabited the island of Crete. The people we call Greeks did not begin arriving until about

Black-Figure Pottery. Warriors battle on the side of this *amphora* (two-handled jar) dating from about 540 B.C. Decorated in black on light-colored background, the jar is a fine example of the black-figure pottery developed in Athens and very popular until it was supplanted in 525 B.C. by red-figure pottery. At this point in the evolution of Greek art, the two warring figures are still stylized. But black-figure pottery was beginning to take on some form of realism, associated with the best Greek art.

1900 B.C. They seem to have come from the Balkan region now called Bulgaria.

These migrating people gradually moved north, carrying their language with them; it became the German language. They also moved west into Italy, where their language became that of the Romans. They moved south, where their language became Greek. They moved east across the Himalayas into India, where their language was preserved in Sanskrit. These wanderers with their *Indo-European* language provided a common ancestry for scores of civilizations. Words that still remain in the languages of widely separated countries reveal their single source.

The first group of this great family arrived in the Greek peninsula about 1900 B.C. and were called Achaeans. Some settled in the Plains of Thessaly. Others moved to the southernmost part of the land called the Peloponnesus. By 1200 B.C. King Agamemnon of Mycenae, a powerful city-state in the northeast section of the Peloponnesus, emerged as the foremost leader of these settlements. Agamemnon led an attack force to Troy on the Asian shore of the Aegean Sea. His destruction of Troy opened the door for more Achaeans to migrate to Asia Minor, where they set up cities of Greek-speaking peoples.

The Achaeans' migration to Asia Minor was probably prompted by invasions of more tribes from the Balkans. The Dorians moved into Greece over a period of three centuries (1500–1200 B.C.). They too spoke a form of Greek, but they were hostile to the settled peoples of the Greek peninsula. They burned Mycenae and other cities, including Cnossus in Crete (the center of the Minoan civilization). Thus they destroyed the culture and commerce that had steadily developed over about 2000 years.

However, the Ionians moved to the eastern side of the Aegean and preserved their heritage. They spread north and south along the rim of Asia Minor in a region eventually called Ionia. Homer, the great Greek poet, produced his literary masterpieces there sometime between 900 and 700 B.C.

The next people to invade and settle Greece were the Aeolians, who occupied west central Greece, the northern Peloponnese, and the islands offshore. The exact time at which these invaders appeared in Greece is uncertain.

While Greece was being invaded from the Balkans over a period of about 8 centuries (1900–1100 B.C.), the Israelites were developing into a nation. This period spans the time of the patriarchs Isaac and Jacob, Israel's stay in Egypt and the Exodus (1446 B.C.), the conquest of Canaan (1399 B.C.), and a large portion of the period of the judges, which ended in 1043 B.C. when Saul was made king.

B. Age of the Kings. The next stage in early Greek history can be called the age of the kings (*ca.* 1000–750 B.C.). The waves of new people that surged into Greece often settled in towns and villages with the original inhabitants. Hundreds of valleys and plains provided convenient settlement centers. These city-states were ruled by kings.

The region called Attica included Athens, a city that eventually absorbed the many self-governing townships

Greek War Tactics

Greece's domination of the ancient world and the spread of the Greek language throughout the Mediterranean area are two of the most startling facts of history. Modern Greece is only slightly larger than the State of New York, it is filled with mountains, and its soil is rather unproductive. Ancient Greece knew little political unity. So what was the secret of Greek military success? Here are a few possible answers:

Ancient Greeks were raised to be soldiers. In Sparta, children belonged to the state. Defective boys were thrown out on the hills to die; strong ones were educated by the state, and most education was physical. Boys were taught to run, wrestle, endure pain without flinching, live on reduced rations, obey commands—and to rule. They were also taught mathematics, philosophy, music, and the love of reading.

These qualities can be seen in some famous Greek battles. Feeling it was time to conquer Greece, Darius I of Persia assembled a huge army and 600 ships. Drunk with success (he had just destroyed Miletus), Darius was confident that he could subdue Greece within days.

The Persians landed on the east side of Attica at a place near Marathon. News of the oncoming battle alarmed Greece. Slaves and freemen were enlisted at Athens and forced to march across the mountains to Marathon. By the time the Greeks assembled, there were only 20,000 of them. (The armies of Sparta were delayed and did not arrive in time). The Persians, on the other hand, had 100,000 hardened veterans.

The Persians filled the air with arrows; but they had little effect, for the Greeks were well-armored. Under the leadership of Miltiades, the Greeks attacked as a team. Teamwork was something the Persians did not understand; they fought as individuals.

The battle was a disaster for Darius. According to Greek records, 6,400 Persians lost their lives while only 192 Greeks fell. At the end of the battle, the delayed Spartans arrived and praised the victors. Darius failed to conquer Greece, but his son Xerxes had the same dream; he collected troops and war materials, and by 481 B.C. he was ready. According to Herodotus, this army had 2,641,000 fighting men in addition to slaves, engineers, and others.

As the huge army marched westward toward Greece, it passed through Thrace and by Philippi and Macedonia. Many Greeks on the way surrendered, either because of terror or bribes. These Greeks allowed their armies to become a part of the Persian army.

Rising to the occasion, Themistocles,

around it. Legend says that King Theseus united Attica under Athenian rule, forcing everyone to pay taxes and be enrolled as a citizen of Athens.

Athens became a prominent city-state by about 700 B.C. Others also developed—including Megara, Corinth, Argos, and Sparta to the east and south, and Thebes to the north. The Greek word for city (*polis*) referred to the entire political state ruled by a city.

The city-states constantly quarreled among themselves, sometimes one-on-one and sometimes in groups called *leagues*. In addition to warring, they carried on extensive trading and exploration throughout the Mediterranean and even as far as the British Isles.

commander of the Athenian contingent, requested his sailors to paint huge signs on the rocks that the Persian fleet could see as they passed by. These signs implored the Greeks in the fleet to either desert or refuse to fight against their native land. Themistocles knew that even if the Greek sailors did not desert, Xerxes would be worried about using them.

The rival fleets finally clashed and fought until darkness stopped them. Many Greeks turned traitor and showed the Persians secret passes over their mountains. Undaunted, King Leonidas of Sparta gathered 300 Spartans to guard the pass at Thermopylae. Knowing that this was extremely dangerous, he only chose men who had sons, so that their family names would not be extinguished. Including other garrisons, his army consisted of only 6000 men.

When the fighting got tough, most of the Greeks escaped. But Leonidas and all but two of his Spartans died fighting. The Persians lost 20,000, the Greeks 300. (One of the two Spartan survivors fell later in a battle at Plataea; the other survivor hanged himself to avoid shame.)

The following year, an army of 110,000 Greeks attacked the Persians. Though outnumbered, they killed 260,000 Persians.

One hundred and twenty-three years after the defeat of Xerxes, King Philip of Macedonia had a son named Alexander. Alexander became the greatest Greek general of all times. Inspired by Homer's *Iliad,* he early determined that he would conquer the world. Macedonian training and Alexander's phalanx were vital factors in Greek victories.

There were 9,000 men in a phalanx, divided into squares with 16 men on each side. Each man was protected with armor and a 4-m. (13-ft.) spear. Standing about 1 m. (3 ft.) apart, shields in position, they formed a human tank.

In addition to the phalanx and cavalry, Alexander had war machines designed by Diades, a Greek engineer. These bow-like machines could shoot huge arrows or hurl 22-kg. (50 lb.) stones more than 180 m. (200 yds.). Alexander's army also carried huge towers with which they could scale enemy walls.

Alexander was a master of propaganda. He loved to terrify foes by scattering enormous bridle-bits where they could easily be seen. This gave the impression that he possessed super-sized horses!

So the Greeks used shrewd psychology as well as mechanical genius to conquer their foes. They overcame enormous odds to establish themselves as masters of the Mediterranean world.

During the age of the kings, the Greeks began to develop distinctive patterns of art and commerce. They learned commercial skills from the Phoenicians, who dominated Mediterranean trade at that time. They also borrowed the Phoenician alphabet and added vowels to it. The Greek literature of this period is best preserved in the epic poems known as the *Iliad* and the *Odyssey,* which are usually attributed to Homer.

This period in Greece's history roughly parallels the monarchy of Israel, which began when Saul became Israel's first king in 1043 B.C. and ended when the Assyrians defeated Israel in 722 B.C.

C. The Rise of Democracy. The rule of Greek kings was slowly usurped by nobles, who enjoyed great wealth and

Alexander the Great. This youthful king of Macedonia (*ca.* 356–323 B.C.) changed the world militarily and culturally. He destroyed the Persian Empire and swept through Syria, Palestine, and Egypt, marching as far as India's Ganges River before his tired troops mutinied, forcing him to turn back. Alexander spread the Hellenistic culture and established Greek as the dominant language throughout the known world.

power at the expense of the peasants. This period of injustice set the tone for later Greek religion, and it helped pave the way for reception of the gospel in the Gentile world.

The nobles vanished from the scene by about 600 B.C. and merchants became the most important leaders in the Greek city-states. A system of metal coinage had been adopted in the early 600's, so that wealth was now accumulated in lands, slaves, and money. All of these gains were no help to the poverty-stricken peasants, so the city-states passed laws to limit the power of wealthy tyrants. By 500 B.C., democracy had a strong foothold in Greece.

Greek democracy gave citizens a voice in their own affairs—an innovation in ancient government. There was no sense of citizenship among the Egyptians or Mesopotamians, not even among the Old Testament Jews. When a Hebrew prophet denounced social wrongs, he appealed to the justice of Jehovah rather than the rights of man. The Greeks were the first to develop a system of government that guaranteed civil liberties and focused upon civic obligations.

During this period, Greek culture produced lyric poetry, architecture, sculpture, and religious thought that would continue to affect the world for centuries to come. Pindar,

Tyrtaeus, and Sappho were well-known poets of this period. Greek architects abandoned the flat Egyptian style of construction to design buildings with soaring columns, sloping roofs, and carved friezes. Greek sculptors carved their works in marble that would last through the ages.

Greek gods were no longer thought of as acting unjustly or capriciously. Greek philosophers raised the cry for social justice. They began teaching that the deeds of men would be judged after death in the court of Minos and Rhadamanthus.

While Greece was making these great cultural strides, the Jews were facing a bleak future. The people of Judah were exiled by their Babylonian enemies in 586 B.C. Persia conquered Babylon in 539 B.C., and although Cyrus the Great allowed the Jews to return home, there could be no real resurgence of Jewish nationalism until the time of the Seleucids, who inherited part of the domain of Alexander the Great.

D. The Brief Unification of Greece. The city-states were so jealous of each other and so fiercely independent that they could unite only for brief periods to fight a common enemy. This eventually led to their downfall.

Cyrus the Great conquered Asia Minor and made Persia the strongest military power in the world. A Persian army attempted to invade Greece in 490 B.C., but Athenians defeated them at Marathon. A second Persian invasion by land and sea in 480 B.C. plunged all the way to Athens, which was partially destroyed. It was during this invasion that the Spartan king Leonidas made his heroic stand at the pass of Thermopylae. The Athenians formed a league of city-states and drove out the Persians in 479 B.C., having inflicted a crushing defeat on the Persian navy at Salamis.

E. The Peloponnesian Wars. Because Athens had led this military victory, Athens became the dominant force of the Greek world. Sparta resented this power and pulled Corinth and Megara into a league to squelch Athens. The series of battles between Athens and Sparta came in two phases (459–446 B.C. and 431–404 B.C.), called the Peloponnesian Wars.

This period has also been called the "golden age of Athens." Under Pericles, Athens surpassed its former glory. The buildings of the Acropolis, including the famed Parthenon, belong to this period. The greatest Greek writers lived in the Periclean era—Aeschylus, Sophocles, Euripides, and Aristophanes. The debates of Socrates began the Greek philosophical tradition that Plato and Aristotle were to adorn in the next century. The Athenian fleet ruled the Aegean Sea, and with that superiority came wealth and power.

Yet Sparta defeated Athens in 404 B.C., and the victorious Spartans used ruthless methods to dominate the Hellenic mainland. Corinth, Athens, Argos, and Boeotia formed a league to resist Sparta. But the Corinthian War (as it was called) ended when Sparta made an alliance with Persia. With this extra support, Sparta forced Athens and its allies to recognize Spartan authority over the Hellenic mainland. They agreed upon the Peace of Antalcidas or King's Peace of 386 B.C. This treaty yielded Hellenic cities in Asia Minor to Persian rule, allowed the Aegean islands to remain independent, and placed Sparta in absolute military control of the mainland.

Spartan power did not last long. In 378 B.C., the people of Thebes—a city-state 48 km. (30 mi.) north of Athens—recaptured their citadel. They were led in their battle by a man named Epaminondas, who developed a new military tactic that revolutionized Hellenic warfare. Until this time, battles had been fought in parallel lines, with opposing armies meeting each other head-on in wave after wave of fighting men. Epaminondas created the "oblique order" of battle. He divided his army into two units: one for defense, the other for offense. The offensive wing was strengthened with additional men. While the defensive wing advanced slowly toward the enemy, the offensive wing advanced on the left to break through a given point. The Thebans surprised the Spartan armies with this tactic, crushing Spartan units at Leuctra around 371 B.C. This victory gave Thebes control over Greece.

While Thebes was fighting Sparta, units were mobilizing

160 km. (100 mi.) north of Athens and Thebes in an area called Thessaly. The leader of this growing threat was Jason of Pherae, who turned Thessaly into a powerful armed camp. But he was assassinated before he could move against Thebes.

In 362 B.C., Epaminondas of Thebes gained another victory over the Spartans at Mantinea. However, Epaminondas died in the battle. Thebes could not control Greece without him. Nor was Athens capable of assuming leadership, having been weakened by the Peloponnesian Wars. And Thessaly had lost Jason of Pherae. In short, not one of the city-states was strong enough to unify Greece, and the stage was set for the rise of Alexander the Great of Macedon. This came during the Intertestamental Period, when the Jews under Nehemiah rebuilt the walls of Jerusalem, with Persia's permission.

THE RISE OF THE MACEDONIANS

In 359 B.C. a young man named Philip II became the new king of Macedonia. Before he ascended to the throne, Philip had been captured in a battle with Thebes. While a prisoner, he learned war tactics from Epaminondas and planned his own variation of the oblique order of battle—a variation now known as the *phalanx*.

Philip created a powerful new Macedonian army. His cavalry consisted of about 2,000 horsemen in 8 squadrons. He established the king's bodyguard of both cavalry and foot soldiers and 6 infantry battalions of 1,536 men each. Philip also invented an impressive array of siege engines for storming city walls.

His soldiers were heavily armed. In addition to small shields, helmets, and breastplates, the front line of infantry who led the wedge-shaped phalanx carried 4-m. (13-ft.) spears. The cavalry and other infantrymen carried larger shields, plus short thrusting swords and spears.

To free himself for conquest, Philip made a peace agreement with Athens in 358 B.C. He then quickly conquered the

Macedonian city-states of Amphipolis and Pydna. By 352 B.C. he penetrated south into the Greek peninsula and took Thermopylae, a mere 112 km. (70 mi.) from Athens. In 348 B.C. he made a new alliance with Athens and ended what has been called the "Sacred Wars." During the next 10 years Macedonia established its control over much of the Hellenic peninsula. Macedonia—a nation that the Hellenes had considered to be barbaric—was soon to spread Greek culture across many lands.

The golden age of Greek culture was over by the time Macedonia rose to power. One of the last great political figures was Isocrates (436–338 B.C.). Isocrates was a great orator, and his public speaking swayed political thought in Athens. His passion was the defeat of Persia. Isocrates saw the eastern power as a menace to Hellenic society. He felt the Persians were vile and disgusting, and he spent his life arousing hatred and hostility toward them. His most notable follower was none other than Philip II of Macedon.

A. The Advance of the Hellenistic Empire. It did not take long for the Hellenic city-states to mobilize against the Macedonians. The Athenians and Thebans unified to face them, and in 338 B.C. the two forces engaged in battle. The Macedonians soundly defeated the Hellenic units at Chaeronea and took control of Greece. At this battle a young Macedonian cavalry officer appeared for the first time on the battlefield. He was Philip's son, Alexander.

Philip called a meeting at Corinth of representatives from all the Greek city-states, except Sparta. Delegates to this League of Corinth sat on a council, the *Synhedrion* (cf. Jewish *Sanhedrin*). Representation was based on the population of the districts in the city-states. Philip was elected as the *hegemon* (ruler) of the Hellenic League. For the first time since the Persian Wars, the Hellenic cities were unified under one powerful ruler.

Interestingly, though, the conquered Greeks still considered the Macedonians to be foreigners, largely because the Macedonians did not speak one of the Hellenic dialects. However, the Macedonians soon absorbed the Hellenic cul-

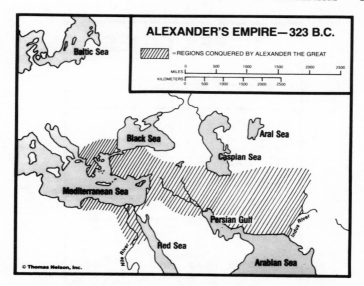

ALEXANDER'S EMPIRE—323 B.C.

= REGIONS CONQUERED BY ALEXANDER THE GREAT

MILES 0 500 1000 1500 2000 2500
KILOMETERS 0 500 1000 1500 2000 2500

Baltic Sea

Black Sea

Aral Sea

Caspian Sea

Mediterranean Sea

Persian Gulf

Indus River

Nile River

Red Sea

Arabian Sea

© Thomas Nelson, Inc.

ture and dialects. Attic Greek—the language spoken in Athens—was adopted as the official language of state under Philip. Thus for the first time on the Hellenic peninsula all the people began to speak a common language. It was called *koine* (meaning "common") Greek. As Alexander marched, this *koine* language went with him, influencing the surrounding communities which he conquered.

B. Alexander the Great. Alexander was born around 356 B.C. His mother was of royal lineage, as was his father, Philip II. When Alexander was 14, he studied under the Athenian philosopher, Aristotle. Perhaps no culture has ever produced a greater mind than Aristotle's. So searching and profound was Aristotle's work that in the twelfth and thirteenth centuries A.D. much of the Christian church regarded his teachings as being divinely inspired. No subject was untouched by his contemplation. Philosophy, botany, geography, zoology, astronomy, and art were all subjects of deep concern for him. Aristotle was the student of Plato and the teacher of Alexander the Great. Either role would have earned him an important place in history.

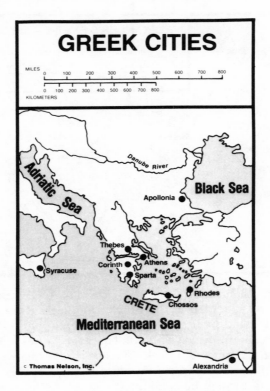

GREEK CITIES

Most likely Aristotle instructed Alexander by reading and discussing Homer and the Greek tragedies. Aristotle also trained Alexander in politics. Through Aristotle, Alexander acquired his deep love for Hellenistic culture, which drove him to the Far East in order to spread the Hellenistic "spirit." Tradition says that Alexander even carried a copy of the *Iliad* throughout his Persian and Oriental campaigns.

One of Alexander's most cherished possessions was the horse he had trained as a youth; it was named Bucephalus. This was his mount in all of his major battles and conquests. The horse died in India, and Alexander built the city of Bucephala on the Hydaspes River in memory of his horse.

In 336 B.C., when Alexander was 20 years old, his father

Philip was assassinated under mysterious circumstances and Alexander was made the new Macedonian king. His rivals spread rumors of Alexander's own death and he spent much of the following year in quelling revolts that these rumors inspired. He destroyed Thebes in the process. This gave him undisputed control over the Hellenic peninsula.

1. The March toward Persia. In spring of 334 B.C. Alexander led his army of 40,000 men across the Dardanelles into Asia Minor and first engaged the Persians at the Granicus River. The Persian advance guard, lightly armed and unaccustomed to Macedonian tactics, was overwhelmed. Alexander had planned only to free the Greek cities then under Persian control, but the resounding victory spurred him to strike at the heart of the empire itself.

This was no madcap venture. Darius III, the Persian king, was a poor leader and his provincial officials were unreliable. The unwieldy empire was ready to fall in pieces.

The victory at the Granicus River quickly opened the towns of Sardis, Ephesus, and Miletus to Alexander's conquest. Miletus was the traditional birthplace of Hellenic philosophy; Sardis and Ephesus would play significant roles in the New Testament church (cf. Rev. 1:11; 3:1, 4).

In 333 B.C., Alexander moved on Gordium, the capital of Phrygia. The goal of this offensive was the Cilician Gates, a narrow mountain pass to Syria and Palestine. Moving through the pass, Alexander advanced onto a plain near the village of Sollioi. The leader of Darius' Greek mercenaries advised the Persian king to keep his forces on the open plain. But Darius established a defensive position on the Pniaurus River. Here would be the first encounter between the Macedonians and the Persian royal units. The phalanxes of the Macedonians again proved too powerful for the Persian army. Darius swiftly retreated, relinquishing Asia Minor to the Macedonian conqueror.

During 332 B.C., Alexander swept through Syria, Palestine, and Egypt. He captured the Phoenician naval base of Tyre, once thought to be invulnerable to attack from land. (The city was on an island, but Alexander built a causeway to it. Some consider this his greatest victory.) Egypt hailed him as the deliverer who freed them from their Persian overlords.

While wintering in the Nile Valley, he chose the site for a new commercial center to take the place of Tyre. Alexandria, as the new city was called, occupied a highly favorable position for linking the trade of the Mediterranean with India and the Far East.

As a result of Alexander's conquests, the center of Western civilization was shifting—culturally and economically. Alexandria replaced the cities of Greece as the focus of Greek intellectual and artistic life.

In 331 B.C., Alexander resumed his eastward march and this was perhaps the most significant period in his career. He crossed the Syrian desert to confront the Persians in one final epic battle. This battle has been given two names, Arbela or Gaugamela. On the open plains, Darius III faced Alexander with the remainder of his armies and a line of battle elephants. Alexander's troops were at first startled by the appearance of the beasts—but not startled enough for this to be of help to Darius III. The Persian king was killed by his own troops as he attempted to flee from the battle. The tactics of phalanx and cavalry again carried the day, and the Macedonians achieved a signal victory. After the battle Alexander was crowned king of Asia. Thus the crusade for Hellenic vengeance was accomplished. The Persian Empire was soundly defeated.[1]

2. Alexander and the Orient. After Alexander defeated Darius III at the Battle of Arbela, he immediately captured the old Persian seats of power in Susa, Babylon, and Ecbatana. He took enough booty in the capture of Susa to finance all of his later expeditions.

Thus the first chapter of the great Hellenistic conquest opened a second chapter.

While in Ecbatana, Alexander decided to explore the Orient. The Persians had long claimed the territories of western India as a part of their empire. Indeed, they had brought their battle elephants from the region of India. However, Alexander's new plan for conquest and exploration was the first known instance of a European's venturing into the mysterious East.

In 330 B.C. Alexander began the march north and east from the capital cities near the Persian Gulf. By 329 B.C. his forces had crossed the Hindu Kush mountains, threading their way through Afghanistan and overrunning the provinces of Bactria and Sogdiana. It took two years to pacify the area. While there, Alexander married Roxanne, a princess of noted beauty.

On this eastward move, Alexander underwent some rather deep personal changes. He began to adopt Persian and Oriental costumes for his dress. He also introduced the Oriental custom of *proskynesis* (Greek, "worship"). In other words, he required his troops to make a display of worship by lying on the ground before him in the Oriental fashion. This rankled the Macedonian units. Though they respected their king, they still regarded him as a mortal being, not a god. Because he opposed this policy, Callisthenes—the historian for Alexander's campaigns and a nephew of Aristotle—was arrested, tried, and executed under Alexander's orders. Perhaps this marks the lowest ebb in Alexander's career.

In the latter part of 327 B.C. Alexander began to move his units south, again crossing the Hindu Kush mountains. As Alexander approached the Indus River, people of the village

Ptolemy I. A general of Alexander the Great, Ptolemy received Egypt as his share of the Greek Empire after Alexander's death. His descendants ruled Egypt from 323 to 30 B.C., infusing the land of pharaohs with Hellenistic culture and running the state on a business basis, with profits payable to the crown. The Ptolemies also controlled Palestine until the Seleucids of Syria wrestled it away.

Golden mask. Heinrich Schliemann discovered this golden death mask in a Greek tomb in Mycenae, Greece in 1876. He thought it was a mask of the face of Agamemnon, a hero in the Trojan War. But the carefully crafted golden artifact actually dates from between the sixteenth and nineteenth centuries B.C., long before the Trojan War.

Taxila met his army with a massive assault of battle elephants. The Macedonians won the battle, but were exhausted and frightened at the prospect of fighting more elephant armies on the other side of the Indus. Alexander's beloved horse, Bucephalus, died during the conflict. The army mutinied and refused to go any farther east. Alexander had no choice but to lead them back across the terrible desert of Gedrosia in present-day Pakistan and Iran.

Alexander returned to Ecbatana, then to his capital city of Babylon, where he began preparations for the conquest of Arabia and the organizing of his empire. Weakened by heavy drinking, he was unable to survive a bout with malaria. He died in 323 B.C. at the age of 32. His body was placed in a beautiful tomb in Alexandria.

3. The Jews under Alexander. According to tradition, Alexander treated the Jews favorably, and they fought in his army. Both the historian Josephus and the Jewish Talmud mention this as they describe Alexander's attack on Tyre. Alexander ordered the Jews to help him with troops and supplies, but the high priest Simon the Just refused because he was loyal to Persia. However, after both Tyre and Gaya fell to Alexander, Simon had a dream that told him to go out with the people and meet the victor. When he did this, Alexander bowed before the divine name on the priest's headdress, because he too had had a dream in which he had seen the headdress. Alexander then worshiped in the temple and granted the Jews a certain amount of self-rule in his territories.

Palestine was included in the province of Coele-Syria, whose governor Andromachus lived at Samaria. Jealous over the privileges that Alexander granted the Jews, the Samaritans revolted and burned the governor to death in his house. In retaliation, Alexander expelled the population of Samaria and settled Macedonians in the city. They rebuilt the old Semite city into an outpost of Greek civilization with a theatre and enormous public buildings.

Deuterocanonical references to Alexander are found in 1 Maccabees 1:1-8; 6:2. Daniel 7 and 11:3-4 also refer to Alexander the Great, and some scholars feel that Zechariah 9:1-8 refers to Alexander's conquest of Palestine.

4. Alexander's Legacy. Alexander's campaigns profoundly influenced subsequent history. His personal achievements were largely military, but he laid the foundations for the cultural development of Western civilization. Alexander's marriage of the Oriental culture of the East and the Hellenic culture of the West can be seen in the fourth and third century B.C. statuary of Gautama Buddha, which bear striking Hellenic characteristics, especially in the faces.

Through his conquests, Alexander managed to spread the language of *koine* Greek among the people of many lands and cultures. The *koine* Greek would come to dominate this portion of the Mediterranean and Oriental regions until the period of the Byzantine Empire (A.D. 395). This common language facilitated the spread of the gospel of Christ during Paul's time. In fact, the earliest New Testament manuscripts were written in this *koine* dialect.

Alexander built several "Alexander" cities along his route of conquest. These cities radiated Greek language, arts, and government. They had a profound impact on their surrounding regions.

5. The Aftermath of Alexander's Death. However, all was not well in the Hellenistic Empire. When Alexander died, he left no successor. His son by Roxanne was not born until after his death, so his field marshals scrambled to claim the lands they had conquered. These generals and their successors, primarily the Ptolemies of Egypt and the Seleucids of Syria, warred among themselves until the Roman conquests began in 197 B.C. These struggles had a profound effect upon the Jews.

Antiochus III of the Seleucid Empire died *ca.* 187 B.C. He was succeeded by his son Antiochus IV (Epiphanes) in 175 B.C. Under his leadership, the Seleucid Empire carried out a thorough Hellenistic reconstruction of its subject lands. Particularly affected by this new campaign were the Jews.

HELLENISM IN PALESTINE

When Antiochus IV inherited the Seleucid part of the Greek Empire in 175 B.C., he had a burning passion to unite all of his territory by spreading Hellenism throughout. Known as one of the cruelest tyrants of all time, he used harsh methods that stirred opposition, particularly in Jerusalem. The city's dwellers were caught between rival and faithless priests who contended for leadership of the city. Antiochus smashed the civil strife, massacred thousands of the people, and robbed the temple of its treasures. The governor that Antiochus left in charge of Jerusalem was also cruel. The people chafed under his control.

INFLUENCE ON BIBLE HISTORY

Not a great deal of Bible history comes to us from the period following the sixth century B.C. Much of the Jewish literature that claims to report on this period has been classified as *apocryphal* ("hidden") and *pseudepigraphical* ("false name") writings. Yet some of these writings fill in the story of this period as seen through Hellenistic eyes. These writings bear evidence of being more Hellenistic than Jewish.

The Jews did not easily give themselves to the ways of their conquerors, such as the Persians and Greeks. Though some nations adopted the customs of their victors, the Jews tried to withstand this temptation.

Not all Jews returned to Judea. Many scattered throughout the Persian Empire, seeking official positions and establishing new communities. This scattering of the Jewish race and culture has been referred to by the Greek word *Diaspora* ("Dispersion").

A rather large Jewish community established itself in Alexandria, Egypt under the Ptolemies. The Ptolemies made certain that their Alexandria was a center of Hellenistic culture equal to Athens. Artwork and literature abounded in this metropolitan city. The architecture of Alexandria was famous—from the towering Pharos lighthouse at the entrance of the eastern harbor to the city's museum and great library. The Ptolemies collected a large quantity of existing literature. The dry desert air of Egypt helped to preserve this great body of ancient literature.

An outstanding literary accomplishment under the Ptolemies was the translation of the Hebrew Scriptures into the *koine* Greek dialect. This translation was called the *Septuagint*. The translation project is said to have been sponsored by Ptolemy II Philadelphus around the third century B.C. According to tradition, 72 Jewish scholars (6 from each tribe) were summoned for the project and the work was finished in 72 days; the Jewish scholars were then sent away with many gifts. This story may be nothing more than a legend; but the translation indeed came out of the Alexandrian determination to preserve the great writings of the time in Greek.

The Septuagint provided a bridge between the thoughts and vocabulary of the Old and New Testaments. The language of the New Testament is not the *koine* of the everyday Greek, but the *koine* of the Jew living in Greek surroundings. Learned men throughout the Mediterranean became acquainted with the Septuagint. By the New Testament era, it was the most widely used edition of the Old Testament.

Alexandrian Jews adopted *koine* Greek as their language. In their attempt to persuade their gentile neighbors that the God of the Jews was the one true God, they used *koine* diction, Hellenistic literary patterns, and gentile thought-forms. All of these are reflected in the Septuagint and many other Jewish

The Parthenon

The Parthenon in Athens is one of the finest examples of classic Greek architecture. It physically represents the ancient Greeks' rational, harmonious approach to life. Moreover, it is a marvel of architectural design.

The Greeks erected at least one previous structure on the site of the Parthenon in 488 B.C., when they laid out a massive structure as a thank-offering for their victory over the Persians at Marathon. The limestone foundation for this building extended over 6 m. (20 ft.) into the rock of the Acropolis. Most above-ground work on this site was destroyed, however, when the Persians sacked the Acropolis in 480 B.C.

The Greeks began work on the Parthenon in 447 B.C. and completed it in 438 B.C. They made the structure the main temple on the Acropolis around 432 B.C., when they dedicated it to Athena Parthenos, patron goddess of Athens. Construction on this building was funded by the government of Pericles.

The building was designed to create an optical illusion. The tops of the Parthenon's Doric columns lean toward the center of each colonnade, the steps curve upward at the center, and the columns are more widely spaced at the center of each row than at the end. This makes the columns appear to be evenly spaced. (If they had truly been evenly spaced, the perspective angle would have made them look uneven.)

There are eight columns at each end of the Parthenon and seventeen on each side. The Parthenon has a central area, or *cella*, which in turn is divided into chambers. An inner colonnade originally held the great cult statue of Athena, a masterpiece of the sculptor Phidias. This statue has not survived, but we know of its general appearance through smaller copies and through many representations on ancient coins. This statue was seen and described by Greek traveler Pausanias in the second century A.D.

The entire Parthenon is made of marble, including the tiles on the roof. The Greeks used no mortar or cement on the structure; they fitted marble blocks together with the greatest accuracy and secured them with metal clamps and dowels.

An ornamental band of low relief sculpture (*frieze*) decorates the Parthenon. These decorations represent combat among the gods such as Zeus, Athena, and Poseidon. They also picture mounted horsemen, chariot groups, and citizens of Athens.

The Greeks used color to highlight the Parthenon's beauty. The ceiling of the colonnade was colored with red, blue, and gold or yellow. A band running next to the frieze was colored red, and color accented the sculpture and bronze accessories within the Parthenon.

The Parthenon had a varied history. As early as 298 B.C., Lachares stripped the gold plates from the statue of Athena. In A.D. 426 the Parthenon was converted into a Christian church, and the Turks turned it into a mosque in 1460. In 1687 the Venetians, who were battling the Greeks, used the Parthenon as a powder magazine, and accidentally set off an explosion that destroyed the central section of the building. No major repairs were made until 1950, when engineers put fallen columns back in place and repaired the northern colonnade.

writings, such as Philo's *Against Flaccus* and the *Embassy to Caligula*. Hellenism also influenced the writing of Second and Third Maccabees and the New Testament. The Jewish writer Philo Judaeus was the leading philosophical thinker of the time. He said the God of Israel was the God of the philosophers, and he equated the teachings of Hebrew Scriptures with the ideologies and ethics of Greek philosophy, Platonism in particular.

Alexandria also played an important role in early Christendom. A Christian school there was headed by such famous church fathers as Clement and Origen; it flourished from the second to the late fourth century A.D. The school taught that Scripture had three meanings: the literal, the moral, and the spiritual. The most vital of these was the spiritual meaning, and the school's use of allegory for biblical interpretation surpassed the complexity of similar methods used by earlier Hellenistic Jews.

Antiochus IV returned to Jerusalem in 168 B.C. and destroyed the city, killing most of the men and selling the women and children into slavery. Only a few men escaped into the hills under the leadership of Judas Maccabeus.

Maccabeus staged a revolt that secured a brief period of independence for Judea. The books of 1 and 2 Maccabees give a detailed description of this struggle, in which the Judeans formed an alliance with Rome. This backlash in Judea brought the eventual collapse of the remaining Hellenistic kingdoms under the growing power of Rome.

By 165 B.C. the Greek rulers had been driven from Palestine. Judea proper was ruled by the high priest, the leading figure in the Jewish religion and society. The new Judean state was dominated by the officials of the religious cult.

Around 143 B.C. Simon, a descendant of the Maccabees, was named both high priest and ethnarch. (*Ethnarch* was a position very much like that of a medieval vassal king. He was the royal ruler of a given district; however, his rule was authorized by one who ruled the larger region of which his district was a member.) Simon and the Maccabeans resisted attempts to make Judea a Hellenistic state. But their efforts were only partially successful. Judea soon found itself under the rule of the wealthy Sadducee sect, a high priestly group who tended toward Hellenizing influences. (For a thorough discussion of the Pharisees and Sadducees, *see* chapter 5, "Jews in New Testament Times.")

The subtle Hellenizing influence entered many areas of Palestinian life. Architecture was one of those areas. The Jerusalem temple built by Herod the Great was one of the best examples of Hellenism in local architecture. The temple was built like other eastern Hellenistic temples; it stood within a network of courts surrounded by porticoes with freestanding Corinthian colonnades.

The city of Caesarea, which became the official capital of Palestine under the procurators, had buildings that were characteristic of a Hellenistic city: a theater, an amphitheater, a colonnaded street, a hippodrome (an arena for racing), and a temple.

It is hard to identify original Jewish art, for it was so strongly influenced by Hellenism. Also, we must remember that the Law of Moses forbade the making of any graven images (Exod. 20:4). This inhibited the Jews from developing any notable works of pictorial art.

INFLUENCE ON THE NEW TESTAMENT

The New Testament refers to some Christians as "Hellenists" (Acts 6:1; 9:29 RSV). We do not know exactly what this meant. (Some scholars believe that these people were Jews of the *Diaspora* who had adopted a Hellenistic lifestyle.) At any rate, other Christians snubbed these Hellenists in distributing aid to widows (Acts 6:1ff.); and the tension between the Hellenists and other Christians threatened to divide the early church. The apostles overcame this problem by appointing seven deacons, including the Hellenistic leader Stephen, to supervise the distribution of goods.

Some commentators believe that Hellenistic Christians did much of the early missionary work in Gentile lands (cf. Acts

8:1-3; 11:19-30). This would have been a logical development, but Scripture does not give us concrete proof that it happened this way.

We find a number of Hellenistic influences in Paul's letters. It seems that Paul absorbed a considerable amount of Greek wisdom during his years in Tarsus, for he was able to express the gospel in terms that the Greek mind could readily understand.

Throughout his letters, Paul tries to articulate the "deep things of God" (1 Cor. 2:10). He frequently used Greek philosophical concepts to do this. For example, he described how Christ united Gentiles and Jews in "one new man" who could come into fellowship with God (Eph. 2:15). He spoke of Christ "being in the form of God," yet taking "the form of a servant" (Phil. 2:6-7) or being "the image (i.e., the visible expression) of the invisible God" (Col. 1:15). These statements struck fire in the minds of Greek readers who were well-acquainted with Plato's teachings about visible forms and invisible ideals.

At times, Paul interpreted Old Testament events in an allegorical way, as Hellenistic Jewish writers commonly did. The best example is his interpretation of the story of Sarah and Hagar. He explained that their experience was an allegory of people who still lived under the Old Covenant while others lived under the New Covenant of Christ (Gal. 4:21-31). As we have seen, Hellenistic thinkers at Alexandria later developed this method of interpretation to its height.

Yet Greek philosophy did not provide the *substance* of Paul's teachings. Paul differed sharply with the Greek thinkers; in fact, he was sometimes hostile toward them. He told the Colossians, "Beware lest any man spoil you through philosophy and vain deceit, after the tradition of men, after the rudiments of the world, and not after Christ" (Col. 2:8).

The classical scholar William M. Ramsay noted that "the influence of Greek thought on Paul, though real, is all purely external. Hellenism never touches the life and essence of Paulinism . . . but it does strongly affect the expression of Paul's teaching. . . ."[2]

A ROMAN WORLD; A GREEK CULTURE

After Judea fell to the Romans in 63 B.C., Egypt was the only remnant of the Hellenistic kingdoms. Egypt lasted as a sovereign state until 31 B.C., when the Roman generals Octavian (Augustus) and Mark Antony fought the Battle of Actium. Mark Antony had married the Ptolemaic queen Cleopatra; thus his defeat brought Egypt under the effective control of Rome.

The Roman forces brought military and governmental unity to the fractured Hellenistic Empire. Rome became the center of government. The formal naming of Augustus as Roman emperor in 27 B.C. signaled the end of the Hellenistic period and the beginning of the Roman imperial period.

Greece was no longer a political power; but its culture and spirit formed the foundations of imperial Roman culture. As the Roman writer Horace observed, "Captive Greece captivated her conqueror." Hellenistic art, literature, and government thrived throughout most of the Roman period. Even *koine* Greek remained the official language of business in the Near East, and New Testament literature was written in this dialect.

Two Greek schools of philosophy flowered during the Roman period. Each offered a path to personal happiness, but their paths went in opposite directions. The Stoics felt that the body should be controlled, denied, even ignored in order to free the mind. Epicureans taught that the body must be satisfied if the mind was to know happiness. Thus the philosophers of Alexandria perpetuated the spirit and culture of fifth-century Athens. In so doing, they perpetuated the spirit of ancient Greece.

4

THE ROMANS

The people of Rome developed the last great civilization of the ancient world. They based their culture in the land now known as Italy, but expanded to cover most of the known world. They were to have a significant impact upon Palestine in the Intertestamental and New Testament eras.

EARLY HISTORY (3000–1000 B.C.)

Around 3000 B.C., tribes from different areas of Europe and Asia formed small towns and farming communities in mountain pockets of the Italian peninsula. The rough shape of the Apennine Mountains allowed many of these small tribes to exist separately. Some of them had migrated to Italy from areas north of the Black and Caspian seas. Historians call these people *Indo-Europeans*—that is, they came from Europe, southwest Asia, and India. Many of these Indo-Europeans were influenced by the Greek culture of their time.

Among them were the Etruscans, who came from the area of Asia Minor that is occupied by modern Turkey. By about 800 B.C. (when Jehoahaz was on the throne of Israel and Joash on the throne of Judah), the Etruscans had formed the first city-state in Italy. We know very little about the Etruscans, except that they made tools and weapons with copper, bronze, and iron. They gained control of the city now called Rome about the sixth century B.C. during the time of the Exile of the Jews.

While the Etruscan culture was developing on the western side of the Apennines, Phoenicians had begun to move across the Mediterranean Sea. Their homeland was on the sea coast of northern Syria. The Phoenicians built a great city-state at Carthage on the northern coast of Africa, across from Sicily. Historians call this the *Punic* civilization (from the Latin word *Punicus*, "of Carthage").

About this same time Greece controlled colonies in Sicily, Sardinia, and southern Italy. The Greek territory in Italy was called *Magna Graecia*, or "Great Greece."

THE RISE OF THE ROMAN REPUBLIC (750–133 B.C.)

While the Greeks and Phoenicians tried to resist the Persians, they lost their grip on the Mediterranean lands. The city of Rome arose in this political setting.

Rome's birth is clouded in legend. One legend said the Trojan warrior Aeneas founded Rome after the fall of Troy in the 1100's B.C. Another legend maintained that two of his descendants, Romulus and Remus, founded Rome in 753 B.C. This would have been while Azariah (Uzziah) ruled Judah and Zachariah and Shallum ruled Israel.

Archaeologists tell us that Rome was much like other tribal centers of its time, though it was older. According to tradition, Etruscan kings ruled Rome until unified Latin tribes drove out Tarquinius Superbus, the last king, in 510 B.C. (This would have been 6 years after the completion of the second temple in Jerusalem.) This rebellion established the Roman republic. Under this republic, there were two classes of citizens—*patricians* and *plebeians. Patricians* were persons of nobility or higher social rank; *plebeians* were people of lower class. The republic assigned two judges to decide civil cases for the patricians, while the plebeians elected tribunes to serve as their officials. Rome suffered from the intense class struggle between patricians and plebeians.

Rome absorbed small Latin kingdoms that surrounded it, but continued fighting with Etruscans in the north and Greek cities in the south. In time, Rome formed a policy that was to be carried through the building of its empire. As it absorbed other peoples, either peacefully or by war, it granted them citizenship and treated them as allies. Rome even absorbed some major Greek colonies, such as Naples, in this manner. Rome controlled all of central Italy by 400 B.C., and began to use its citizen-soldiers against the Greeks of the south. (This was about the time Ezra brought the Law to Jerusalem.) The Romans learned how to read and write from the Greeks, and how to appreciate the finer points of culture and society.

A. Early Warfare. While the Greeks and Phoenicians fought the Persian Empire, they drew their troops away from the Western Mediterranean. Rome grew stronger in the absence of foreign power, basing its strength on the citizen-soldier. The Roman army trained its men to act according to standard rules. Every commander, archer, and foot soldier knew exactly what was expected of him. Roman warfare required many dams, defense walls, and weapons; often these

TRIBES ENTERING ITALY—1500 B.C.

© Thomas Nelson, Inc.

Romulus and Remus. According to legend, Rome was founded by Romulus, a son of the god Mars and a woman named Rhea Silvia. Rhea had taken vows of virginity. As punishment for her violation of the vows, her twin infants Romulus and Remus were abandoned on the banks of the flooding Tiber River. There a she-wolf found and suckled them. On reaching manhood in 753 B.C., Romulus traced the outline of Rome with a plow and became its first king.

preparations took more time and effort than the actual battle. A universal draft provided a constant supply of fresh troops for the Romans. This well-drilled army was also used to build excellent roads and *aqueducts*—bridge-walls used to transport water from the mountains to Roman cities. These projects allowed the Romans to move from one area to another faster than ever before.

During this early period of Rome's growing power, the Romans engaged in constant warfare. The Gauls invaded Italy in 390 B.C. and occupied Rome for 7 months. They left only after receiving a large ransom from the Romans. Then in 340 B.C. (the Intertestamental Period for the Jews), the Romans fought off an invasion by the Latin League, their former allies who had become jealous of Rome's power. Rome also had to conquer the Samnites, a tribe in the central Apennines, in 290 B.C.

Then Rome was ready to challenge the wealthy cities of *Magna Graecia*. While the successors of Alexander the Great fought over the division of his vast conquests, the Romans conquered the Greeks of southern Italy. By 270 B.C., Romans controlled all of Italy.

B. Foreign Wars. The people of Carthage had contended with the Greeks for control of Sicily for over a century. Now the Greek ruler of Syracuse invited Rome to join him in the fight for control. For the next 64 years (264–201 B.C.), Rome fought a series of long wars with Carthage known as the Punic Wars. The Romans finally defeated the famous Carthaginian general Hannibal in 201 B.C. After adding Spain to its conquests, Rome turned to the east.

The Grecian kings of Syria (the Seleucids) and of Egypt (the Ptolemies) constantly fought over the small state of Judea. The Seleucids and Ptolemies went to war against one another in 169 B.C. At the same time, Rome sought to conquer Greece. Rome wanted to avoid a Seleucid rule in both Syria/Palestine and Egypt, so it sent ambassadors to make a pact with the Seleucid ruler, Antiochus IV.

Even as he battled Egypt, Antiochus IV learned of a revolt by the Jews in Jerusalem. He was forced to return to Jerusalem, where he set up a Greek image in the Jewish temple and slaughtered thousands of the Jews (1 Macc. 1:44-64). A Jewish priest named Mattathias, of the house of Hasmon, took to the hills with his five sons and began a revolt. Mattathias' third son was Judas Maccabeus, who led a series of raids against Antiochus (1 Macc. 3:1-9, 42-60; 4:1-61). By 160 B.C., the leaders of the house of Hasmon, called Hasmoneans, were accepted as rulers of Judea.

THE ROMANS ENTER JUDEA (166–67 B.C.)

Much of what we know of the Roman conquest of Judea comes from the *History of the Jewish Wars,* by the Jewish statesman and soldier Flavius Josephus. This history opens with the conquest of Jerusalem by Antiochus IV (Epiphanes) in 170 B.C. and ends with the final victory of the Romans in A.D. 70.

While the leaders of the Hasmon family had gained a measure of self rule, they held office by permission of the Seleucids. The Book of the Maccabees tells of the Jews' rejoicing over Hasmonean victories—but they were small, unimportant victories. The Jews were not a real threat to the

Seleucids; the Greek rulers had more to fear from the Parthians, people from the area now called Iran. The Parthians inherited much of Persia after that empire fell to Alexander the Great. They raided and threatened the Seleucids in the north and east, and later fought many wars with the Romans.

A. Hasmonean Rule. During the rule of the Hasmon family, devout Jews had strong disagreements with those who accepted Greek ways. The Hasmoneans combined the offices of king and high priest in one family. To maintain this double role, they had to balance carefully the various sects of Judaism. The Hasmoneans appealed to the Roman Senate in 161 B.C. for defense against the Seleucids and Ptolemies (1 Macc. 8). Rome promised to aid the Hasmon family and their people in the event they were attacked.

The true Hasmonean line of kings began with John Hyrcanus, who became head of state after the murder of his father and his brothers Mattathias and Judas (1 Macc. 16:16) in 135 B.C. Hyrcanus captured the area of Galilee and the southern area known as Edom (or Idumea). He made Antipater the governor of Galilee and forced all of the surrounding people to become Jews.

Hyrcanus' successors were not as capable of ruling the enlarged Judea. They were influenced more by Greece than by their Hebrew background, and they took on the ways and ideas of late Greek culture. Hyrcanus' eldest son, Aristobulus, succeeded his father in 104 B.C. Aristobulus died within a year; but before he did, he pushed Judea's borders into Galilee, which had been known as "Galilee of the Gentiles." Aristobulus' widow, Salome Alexandra, married Aristobulus' younger brother, Alexander Janneus. Janneus then became king and high priest. He further extended the borders of Judea and severely persecuted the Pharisees, causing a civil war that lasted 6 years. When he died, his widow Salome ruled in his place for the next 7 years. Salome supported the Pharisees and separated the offices of ruler and high priest. She died in 69 B.C.

B. Julius Caesar. Until this time, the Romans had been primarily concerned with the two Greek-influenced kingdoms of the Seleucids and Ptolemies. Historians tell us that major changes now occurred. In defeating Carthage, Rome became master of all the former Semitic colonies—the areas previously called Akkad, Babylonia, Assyria, Phoenicia, and Canaan. Rome also adopted two major Punic traditions: the building of enormous plantations worked by slaves, and the use of cruel measures such as crucifixion to keep the slaves under control. The spread of plantations forced many private Roman farmers from their land and into the city of Rome. The old republican government could not rule the widespread colonies Rome was taking on; a stronger executive rule was needed.

The first person to grab this absolute power was the general

The Senate House. Built in the Roman Forum at the time of Diocletian (*ca.* A.D. 300), this building housed the Roman Senate. During the imperial period, the Senate fell under the domination of the emperors and lost most of its powers.

Julius Caesar (100–44 B.C.). A brilliant soldier and statesman, Caesar extended Rome's border north to the Rhine River and west to Britain. Between 49 and 45 B.C., he eliminated his political rivals to become sole ruler of Rome. His appetite for power led to his assassination in 44 B.C.

named Julius Caesar. He showed the advantages of befriending the tribal peoples on Rome's borders, and he made popular appeals to quiet the mobs in Rome. Julius Caesar was the model of today's popular politician. He was a brilliant, able leader who proved his strength by extending Rome's border north to the Rhine and west to Britain.

Rome's chief ruler in the east was the general named Pompey. He cleared the Mediterranean of pirates and defeated Mithridates IV, the king of Pontus in Asia Minor. Pompey captured the coast of Syria/Palestine, and in 63 B.C. he stormed Jerusalem. Pompey captured Jerusalem's ruler, Aristobulus II, and ended the independent rule of the Hasmon family. Aristobulus II was pulled through the streets of Rome behind Pompey's chariot. Pompey released many of the Hasmonean territories from Jewish control and divided the kingdom of Judea into five districts: Jerusalem, Gadara, Amathus, Jericho, and Sepphoris.

THE FIRST TRIUMVIRATE

In 59 B.C., Caesar, Pompey, and Crassus (a rich real estate speculator) joined forces to form a triple leadership called the First Triumvirate. The rulers of Rome's states and colonies suspected that one man would soon emerge as the complete ruler. Antipater, ruler of Idumea, played one ruler against the other to seek favor. In 54 B.C., Crassus invaded Jerusalem and stole the temple treasure while war broke out between Pompey and Caesar. Antipater sided with Pompey until Pompey was defeated, then switched his loyalty to Caesar. Caesar abolished the five districts and named Antipater procurator of all Judea in 47 B.C. Antipater was killed in 43 B.C., shortly after Caesar's own death.

Caesar's friend, Antony, defeated Caesar's enemies in northern Greece. He then named Antipater's sons, Herod and Phasael, as *tetrarchs* ("rulers of fourths") of Galilee (cf. Matt. 14:1; Luke 3:1,19). When the Parthians invaded Syria/

Greek and Roman Schools

The ancient Romans and Greeks had a sophisticated system of schools. The schools were not compulsory, nor were they run by the government. Still, schooling was popular.

In the Greek system, boys were sent to school at age six. The school was owned and operated by the teacher. Apparently the Greeks did not have boarding schools.

The Greeks did not teach foreign languages. (They considered their language to be supreme!) Their education had three main divisions: music, gymnastics, writing. All Greek children were taught to play the lyre. Greek girls were taught to read and write by their mothers, who also taught them to weave, dance, and play a musical instrument. Oddly, the few well-educated Greek women were usually prostitutes for the wealthy.

Greek lecturers earned a living by teaching in school halls and even on the streets. Some of these wandering teachers—Socrates, for example—became famous. Greek boys could attend school until they were sixteen. After that, they were expected to train in sports.

Unlike the Greeks, the Romans used other nationalities to teach their children. Often a Greek nurse started a child's training. Boys and girls entered formal school at age seven. At thirteen, if they had done well, children went to high school; there were twenty such schools in Rome in A.D. 30. Even Roman secondary education was taught in Greek, and the teachers generally Greek slaves or freedmen. Like the Greeks, the Romans had more advanced teachers who traveled from school to school.

Palestine in 40 B.C. to aid a Hasmonean attempt to regain power, Herod fled to his fortress at Masada on the western shore of the Dead Sea. His older brother, Phasael, was captured and committed suicide.

Herod traveled to Rome, where the Roman Senate named him king of Judea. Antony and his troops finally overpowered the Parthians and their Seleucid allies, and Antony settled in Jerusalem in 37 B.C.

The strain of imperial expansion was so great that Rome took in no new territories for at least 50 years after Caesar's birth. Rome ruled most of Greece, Syria, Judea, and North Africa. Only one Greek-influenced nation remained intact. This was Egypt, ruled by Queen Cleopatra.

THE SECOND TRIUMVIRATE

Cleopatra became Julius Caesar's friend after he defeated Pompey. When Caesar was murdered, Cleopatra tried to pick the winner in the struggle for power that followed. The major contenders were Antony, Lepidus (who had served under Julius Caesar), and Caesar's nephew and adopted son, Octavian. These three kept a temporary peace by forming another triple dictatorship, the Second Triumvirate.

Antony met Cleopatra in 41 B.C. in Cilicia, a region in southern Asia Minor. Cleopatra was neither a ravishing beauty (as modern stories would have us believe) nor an Egyptian. She was Macedonian, and a crafty politician who sought to preserve her kingdom at all costs. Cleopatra married Antony and plotted with him to rule the Roman Empire.

When civil war broke out between Antony and Octavian, Cleopatra convinced Antony to send Herod to fight the Arabians (Nabateans), instead of supporting Antony. She hoped that each nation would weaken the other; Egypt could then absorb both. This move saved Herod's kingdom, for Octavian crushed the forces of Antony and Cleopatra at the Battle of Actium in 31 B.C. and ordered their deaths.

THE JEWS UNDER ROME

In early 30 B.C., Herod met with Octavian and bargained to keep his life and throne. Through the years, Herod had rid himself of any possible claimants to the throne. He had "playfully" drowned his young brother-in-law Aristobulus, executed his uncle Joseph as an adulterer, and framed Hyrcanus II for plotting with the Nabateans. Herod was subject to deep moods of depression, when he would order the murders

---

Pax Romana

Historians have given the title *Pax Romana* ("the Roman peace") to the period from 30 B.C. to about A.D. 180, when Rome flourished in a time of imperial greatness. During this period, the Roman Empire brought peace, prosperity, and good government to an area that ranged from Britain to the Euphrates, and from the North Sea to the Sahara.

The Pax Romana began with the rule of Octavian, who became emperor of Rome after defeating the last of his opponents for that title in the Battle of Actium in 31 B.C. After a century of civil strife, Rome was at last united under one ruler. Octavian, given the title *Augustus* by a respectful Roman Senate, concentrated on his empire's internal problems and laid the foundation for two centuries of strong rule and peace.

The Pax Romana brought a great increase in Rome's trade and prosperity. The imperial navy swept the Mediterranean of pirates who imperiled shipping between Rome, the provinces in Asia Minor, and the African coast. The great Roman roads were built primarily as military routes to the provinces. But they also allowed grain to be brought to the city of Rome, and wine and olive oil to be brought to outer provinces. Tolls and many other artificial barriers to trade were removed. A stable coinage and improved methods of banking and credit encouraged economic expansion. Manufacturing sprang up in Roman provinces, and soon pottery from Gaul, textiles from

Flanders, and glass from Germany could be found in Rome.

A key to the maintenance of peace was Augustus' willingness to allow provinces local self-government, coupled with his quick use of military force to stifle rebellion or terrorism. Augustus allowed conquered nations to keep their language, customs, and religion, as long as the people stayed on peaceful terms with Rome.

Agriculture remained the basic economic activity in the Roman Empire under the Pax Romana, but this period also saw the rapid increase of cities and the creation of a cosmopolitan world-state, where races and cultures intermingled. At its height the Roman Empire had over 100 million people, including Italians, Greeks, Egyptians, Germans, Celts, and others. By the time of Hadrian (reign A.D. 117–138), the empire covered an area of over 1¼ million square miles.

Augustus funneled the wealth of his provinces to Rome through taxes. He rebuilt Rome from a city of bricks to a city of marble. The state also supported many artisans, who belonged to *collegia,* or guilds. Recreations and sports came to play an increasingly large role in the public lives of Roman citizens.

The Pax Romana had come to an end by the time of Rome's real money crisis in the third century A.D., when political anarchy and monetary inflation caused the collapse of the empire's economy.

of friends and family. For example, he ordered the execution of his favorite wife, Mariamne, then brooded over her death.

Herod broke many of the Jewish laws. He introduced Greek-style games and races to his kingdom and ordered many large building projects. Among these were Greek temples, forts, and a palace. His greatest project was a new temple in Jerusalem, which he began in 20 B.C. (Matt. 4:5; 24:1; Mark 11:27; 13:1; Luke 19:45; 20:1; John 2:14).

In 27 B.C., Octavian took the title *Augustus* and ruled the Roman Empire. Augustus Caesar brought peace to the Roman Empire through strict control of his army and land; he created the image of Rome's golden age. (Jesus was born during the rule of Augustus, who died in A.D. 14.)

In 22 B.C., Herod sent his children to Rome to be educated and pay respect to Augustus. Augustus visited Syria in 20 B.C. and gave Herod even more land. Fearing revolt, Herod banned large public gatherings during the visit.

The Colosseum. Between A.D. 72 and 80, the Emperors Vespasian and Titus built the Colosseum, a massive structure with rising tiers of seats circling an open space. Gladatorial battles—fights between animals, and between men and animals—were favorite sports of the Roman spectators. A vast network of underground tunnels provided spaces for the caged animals and human participants, who fought to the death in the arena. The Roman engineers even devised a method to flood the arena for mock sea battles.

Caesar Augustus (63 B.C.–A.D. 14). Grand nephew and adopted son of Julius Caesar, Octavian took the honorary title *Augustus* (i.e., "the exalted") when he became sole ruler of Rome after defeating Mark Antony at Actium. (*Augustus* became the official title for later emperors of Rome.) The reign of Augustus Caesar was a period of peace and prosperity for the empire.

Herod had to deal with the power of Greek-influenced officials in Asia, as well as the power of Augustus in Rome. Herod's other problem was the discontent of Jewish sects and parties. He remembered how the Maccabees had driven Greek sympathizers from their temple in Jerusalem in 165 B.C. He determined to prevent this kind of revolution.

Judaism was the only religion to survive the strong influence of Greek ways. Through the translation of the Old Testament into Greek, Judaism actually increased its influence during the Hellenistic Age. But Judaism's popularity attracted Herod's envy. Though he was not of Jewish birth, he spent large sums of money on the new temple in hopes of winning the Jews' loyalty.

But plots and counterplots marked the last years of Herod's reign. In all, Herod married 10 wives, and his many sons fought for his throne. Time and again, Herod promoted a

Roman Citizenship

During the New Testament era, Rome ruled the Mediterranean world. Its dominion stretched north to the borders of barbaric Gaul (France) and Germany, and encircled the Mediterranean Sea. Egypt was in its grip, as well as the cities of northern Africa.

Yet wherever Romans went, they brought good roads and public works, government officials, soldiers, and sometimes entire colonies of Roman citizens. Despite talks of Roman brutality, Rome was not a vengeful conqueror. Its aim was to make good Romans out of its new subjects, so that the Roman Empire would be truly Roman. This was quite a challenge, because the conquered people burned with hatred toward Rome.

The Roman Senate decided to allow an area as much self-rule as prudence permitted. In Judea, this meant that the native king (Herod the Great) was allowed to rule the Jews. When he died, the kingdom was divided among his three remaining sons: Philip, Archelaus, and Herod Antipas. Jewish nationalists did not accept this, and they finally appealed to Augustus Caesar to abolish the kingship in Judea. This he did in A.D. 6. Though Palestine was still thick with Roman soldiers and tax collectors, Jews were allowed to manage their own internal disputes.

Rome also consolidated the empire by granting Roman citizenship to certain non-Romans. "Never before or since," says historian Will Durant, "has citizenship been so jealously guarded or so highly prized."[1] A man holding Roman citizenship had ties to the ruling elite, though he might be an otherwise unimportant person. Under Rome's tolerant laws, a person could hold dual citizenship. Thus Paul the apostle could enjoy the civic rights of both Tarsus and Rome.

The benefits of Roman citizenship were clear. Roman citizenship was valued not only for the right to vote, but for the protection it afforded. A Roman citizen could not be bound or imprisoned without a trial. He could not be scourged—the common means of wringing a confession from a prisoner. If he felt he was not receiving justice under local rule, he could appeal to Rome.

No wonder Roman authorities in Philippi quaked when they realized that Paul and Silas were not just a pair of rabble-rousing Jews! These men insisted they were Roman citizens, a matter which could be confirmed by a simple check of the census rolls. Emperor Claudius executed men who falsely claimed Roman citizenship; so it was not an assertion to be made lightly. No, the Philippians had unwittingly bound, beaten, and imprisoned Roman citizens. But Paul and Silas were willing to settle for an apology. Paul suggested that since the magistrates had publicly thrown him in jail they could now publicly free him. Gladly the magistrates complied—and begged the wronged missionaries to leave town (Acts 16:12–40).

Later, in Jerusalem, Paul again made use of his "Roman connections." He was taken into protective custody when the howls of his Jewish enemies attracted the Roman militia. When Paul surmised that he was about to be scourged—probably for disturbing the peace—he mentioned his Roman citizenship. Not only did this save him a beating, but it assured him safe passage out of Jerusalem.

The Book of Acts concludes by stating that Paul lived two years in Rome under house arrest. He was permitted to preach and make converts. It is said that Emperor Nero crucified Peter, as common criminals were routinely executed, but Paul was beheaded. This was considered a more honorable and merciful death—the final prerogative of Paul's Roman birthright.

son, discovered a plot, and then killed the son. As he neared his seventieth year, Herod became obsessed with destroying all but his chosen heir. Shortly before his death, he heard the disturbing news that a long-awaited king of Israel had been born in Bethlehem. Herod ordered his soldiers to kill all newborn infants of the Jews, much as he had murdered rivals in his own family (cf. Matt. 2).

Herod lived in Jericho, and he ordered that a number of the Jewish leaders there be killed when he died, so that it would be a time of national grief. Herod had his son, Antipater, killed in early 4 B.C. Five days later Herod himself died. Another of Herod's sons, Archelaus, was left to inherit the throne. Archelaus tried to win over the people through kindness and patience. But rebellion mounted—not so much against Archelaus as against the dead Herod. At Passover a new revolt broke out while Archelaus was on his way to Rome to be confirmed. Roman soldiers looted Herod's temple, and when Archelaus returned many Jews and Samaritans were killed. Rome banished Archelaus from the tetrarchy of Judea and replaced him with a procurator named Coponius in A.D. 6.

Archelaus' younger brother Antipas was tetrarch of Galilee and Perea from 4 B.C. to A.D. 39. He had John the Baptist beheaded, and is often mentioned in the Gospels.

Antipas feared that Jesus was John the Baptist resurrected (Matt. 14:1-2; Mark 6:14-16; Luke 9:7-9). Pharisees warned Jesus to flee the region because Antipas was plotting against Him (Luke 13:31-33). Antipas scornfully tried Jesus during Passion Week, then turned the whole matter over to Pontius Pilate (Luke 23:6-12).

AUGUSTUS ORGANIZES THE EMPIRE

While the family of Herod ruled in Judea, Augustus organized his empire. The Rome he inherited from Julius Caesar was a political hotbed of rival classes and contenders for power. Augustus had seen Caesar's rise to power and the awful way in which Caesar's rule was ended. So Augustus gradually transformed the structure of Roman government to assure his control.

First he introduced a system called the *principate,* which seemed to follow the old republican order and the power of the Senate. It really brought the republic under the personal

Praetorian Guard. This relief shows the Praetorians, who served the Roman emperor as personal bodyguards. The unit was instituted by Augustus, who made them his crack troops stationed in Rome. The Praetorian guard was part of the massive army that expanded the Roman Empire and then policed its boundaries.

control of Augustus. The principate lasted only two years (29–27 B.C.) before it gave way to the empire.

Under the empire, Augustus ruled only a few provinces directly. One of these was Judea. Romans saw Syria/Palestine as a small but troublesome part of their empire.

Augustus brought the *Pax Romana* ("Roman peace") to all provinces within the borders of the empire. There were no major wars within the Roman Empire in the time of Jesus, only minor skirmishes along the borders. But the emperor still relied on his army to keep the peace.

We learn from tomb inscriptions and other writings that troops were drafted from all over the empire and required to become Roman citizens. The legions included Britons, Spaniards, Slavs, Germans, Greeks, Italians, and even Jews. Unfortunate soldiers were assigned to lonely outposts on distant frontiers. We find an example of this in Acts 10:1, which describes the "Italian Cohort" in Palestine. By the time Augustus reached complete power, unrest and civil war had swelled the army to almost 24 legions, or half a million men. Since Rome itself was safe from attack during the early period

How a Roman Road Was Built

The Romans were prodigious road builders. They spent five centuries completing a road system that extended to every corner of their empire and eventually covered a distance equal to ten times the circumference of the earth at the equator. This included over 80,000 km. (50,000 mi.) of first-class highways and about 320,000 km. (200,000 mi.) of lesser roads.

Before the Romans built a road, they conducted a survey. They could calculate distances to inaccessible points, run levels with accuracy, measure angles, and lay out tunnels and dig them from both ends with a vertical shaft. Road surveyors considered the slope of the land and questions of defense. Where necessary (as in the regions of Cumae and Naples), they cut tunnels through mountains with a skill that aroused admiration for centuries. Because Romans tried to build straight roads—often over hills rather than around them—slopes frequently were steep; ten percent grades were common.

When building an important road, Roman engineers dug a trench the full width of the road and 1.2 to 1.5 mi. (4 to 5 ft.) deep. The roadbed was built up with successive layers of large and small stone and rammed gravel; sometimes there was a layer of concrete. Normally roads were surfaced with gravel, which might rest on a bed of mortar. Near cities, in places where traffic was heavy, or in the construction of an important road, engineers paved the surface with large, carefully fitted stones about 30 cm. (12 in.) thick and 45 cm. (18 in.) across.

The type of construction varied with expected traffic, terrain, and available materials. Mountain roads might be only 1.5 to 1.8 m. (5 to 6 ft.) wide, with wider places for passing. Main roads were 4.5 to 6 m. (15 to 20 ft.) wide. The Appian Way was about 5.5 m. (18 ft.) wide—wide enough for two wagons to pass abreast—and paved with basaltic lava.

Stone bridges were usually built where roads crossed streams. Such construction was possible because the Romans had concrete much like that in use today. To make lime mortar set under water and resist water action, the road engineers had to add silica to the mixture. The Romans had large quantities of volcanic sand (*pozzolana*), which had a mixture of silica in proper proportions.

Unfortunately, records do not tell us how long it took to build Roman roads or how large the road gangs were that built them. The Appian Way—"Queen of Roads" and forerunner of many other Roman roads on three continents—was begun in 312 B.C. as a road for use in the Samnite Wars. The 211 km. (132 mi.) to Capua must have been completed within about a decade. Ultimately, the Appian Way reached southward 576 km. (360 mi.) from Rome to Brundisium on the Adriatic Sea. The road system was gradually extended through the efforts of numerous Roman emperors. Augustus, Tiberius, Claudius, and Vespasian were among those who launched great road-building projects.

Some Roman roads have been used throughout the Middle Ages and into modern times. The Appian Way, on which Paul traveled to Rome (cf. Acts 28:13–15), is still an important artery of western Italy. It is a mute reminder of the glory of the time when all roads led to Rome.

of the empire, native Italians usually avoided military service.

The people of conquered colonies saw volunteer service as a path to Roman citizenship and other benefits. The government granted immediate citizenship to army volunteers and paid them a pension on retirement. The military groups made up of non-Romans were called *auxiliaries;* they were about equal in number to the regular army.

Aqueduct. This aerial view of the Roman-built Pont du Gard in Provence, France shows the *aqueduct* (waterway) on the upper level and a roadway on the lower level. The Romans constructed aqueducts to bring running water into their cities from hilly areas outside. The ruins bear testimony to the monumental engineering feats of Rome.

The army was organized as follows: The lowest-ranking active group was the *contubernium* of 8 soldiers, who shared a leather tent that enclosed about 9 sq. m. (30 sq. ft.) in the field. A half *contubernium* (4 men) was assigned for very small work details and patrols. Ten *contubernia* comprised one *century*. While *century* strictly meant 100, a *century* usually consisted of only 70 or 80 men. Six *centuries* made a *cohort*, and 10 *cohorts* made a *legion*. The average Roman legion contained about 6,000 men with their pack animals, cavalry horses, and servants.

Legions were stationed in the two main Roman cities in Palestine: Sebaste (Samaria) and Caesarea, Herod's main seaport (Acts 10:1). This put the legions in much closer contact with Rome. We know that a large number of Roman troops marched up to Jerusalem for the feasts to keep order among the Jewish sects and pilgrims. Jewish sects had few troops, possibly no more than 500, under their command. They also had a semi-military temple guard (probably referred to in Matt. 26:47; John 18:31).

Roman forces in Palestine were still directly under Roman control. A Roman military tribune acted as chief of police and his men were responsible for keeping civil order. These men were stationed in the fortress of Antonia (which guarded Herod's temple) and in Herod's palace (which occupied a prominent spot just south of the modern Jaffa Gate of Jerusalem).

Julius Caesar and Augustus gave Jews a great amount of religious freedom, as the very events of Holy Week attest. (Those events took place during the Jewish observance of Passover.) But relations between Romans and Jews of Judea continued to crumble throughout the first century. Romans still appointed the head of the *Sanhedrin,* the chief Jewish political assembly, and they still chose the Jewish high priest. The Sanhedrin was the religious court of Judaism, and the high priest was the head of the Jewish religious structure (Matt. 26:57-68; Luke 22:66-71; Acts 22:30). To most Roman officials, Jewish religion was too complex to bother with.

The Romans were very practical and they brought many Greek innovations to the marketplace. The Romans surpassed previous cultures in their financial and political success. They developed a thorough code of laws and an elaborate structure

Masada. This aerial view shows the excavated remains of Masada, on the western shore of the Dead Sea. Rebel Jews who camped here killed their women and children and then one another, rather than face capture by Roman troops in A.D. 73.

Emperor Worship

The Romans found many different languages, religions, and cultures among the people they conquered. The Roman Empire gradually absorbed these foreign beliefs, including the worship of political leaders.

The eastern provinces had customs of worshiping their living rulers. Egyptians thought that the pharaohs had descended from the sun god, while the Greeks worshiped their great warriors who had died. Alexander the Great established for himself a cult of worshipers in Alexandria. The Seleucids of Syria and the Ptolemies of Egypt followed this tradition, calling themselves gods living on earth. When the power of Rome began to replace these monarchs, the worship of *Roma* (a deification of the Roman state) began to supplant their cults. The conquered people began to worship great individual Romans—Sulla, Mark Antony, and Julius Caesar.

At first, the Romans disdained this ruler worship. However, they did revere the spirits of their dead ancestors (the *lares*) and the divine spirit of the family head (the *paterfamilias*).

Augustus Caesar combined the ideas of ruler worship and ancestor worship in the imperial cult. In the provinces, his Roman subjects worshiped Roma and Augustus together as a sign of their loyalty to the emperor.

Throughout the empire, Roman subjects incorporated emperor worship into the local religion. In the provinces, leading citizens became priests in the imperial cult to cement their ties with Rome. However, Augustus exempted the Jews from the imperial cult.

The Roman emperor Caligula (A.D. 37–41) proclaimed himself a god; he built two temples for himself—one at public expense, one at personal expense. Dressed as Jupiter, he uttered oracles. Turning the temple of Castor and Pollux into the vestibule of his palace, he appeared between the statues of the gods to receive adoration. He was accused of following the Ptolemaic custom of marrying his sister. In A.D. 40, possibly provoked by the fact that some Jews had destroyed an altar erected to him, Caligula ordered a statue of Jupiter with his own features to be placed in the temple in Jerusalem. The Jews responded by saying that "if he would place the image among them, he must first sacrifice the whole Jewish nation" (Flavius Josephus, *Wars*, Vol. 2, Bk. 10, Sec. 4). The Syrian

---

of officials to enforce those laws. Rome made two basic demands of its people: that they pay taxes and accept the rule of Rome (John 18:19; Rom. 13:1-7). Any rebellion or revolt was met with terrible violence. We see proof of this in the writings of Josephus, as well as in the New Testament (Luke 13:1). But Judea with its vast wastelands had no natural boundaries on three sides, so it was a difficult area for the Romans to police.

The Roman government exercised the power of capital punishment over its colonies, and many Jews were killed as political trouble-makers (cf. Luke 23:18-19). The main conflict between Jews and Romans arose over Roman taxes. The Jews had paid taxes to Rome since 63 B.C. But when Judea was added as a Roman province, Jews were also expected to pay provincial taxes. The Romans thought it wise to choose

governor Petronius succeeded in having the order rescinded.

Claudius, Caligula's successor, restored the religious exemption to the Jews and shunned attempts to worship him. "For I do not wish to seem vulgar to my contemporaries," he said, "and I hold that temples and the like have by ages been attributed to the gods alone."

The most famous account of the policy of the Romans toward the Christians is found in the correspondence between Pliny the Younger (A.D. 62–113) and the emperor Trajan (reign A.D. 98–117). Pliny was sent to Bithynia (modern Turkey) to investigate charges of misgovernment. The Bithynians denounced their Christian neighbors, but Pliny was not sure how to handle them. He told the emperor:

". . . The method I have observed towards those who have been denounced as Christians is this: I interrogated them whether they were Christians; if they confessed it I repeated the question twice again, adding the threat of capital punishment; if they still persevered, I ordered them to be executed. . . . Those who denied they were or had ever been, Christians, who repeated after me an invocation to the gods, and offered adoration, with wine and frankincense, to your image . . . and who finally cursed Christ—none of which acts, it is said, those who are really Christians can be forced into performing— these I thought it proper to discharge . . . For the matter seemed to me well worth referring to you—especially considering the numbers endangered. Persons of all ranks and ages and both sexes are and will be involved in the persecution. For this contagious superstition is not confined to the cities only, but has spread through the villages and rural districts; it seems possible, however, to check and cure it" (Epistle X, 96).

Trajan's reply sums up this policy: "The method you have pursued, my dear Pliny, in sifting the cases of those denounced to you as Christians is extremely proper . . . No search should be made for these people; when they are denounced and found guilty they must be punished; with the restriction, however, that when the party denies himself to be a Christian, and shall give proof that he is not (that is, by adoring our gods) he shall be pardoned on the ground of repentance" (Epistle X, 97).

Emperor worship continued as the official pagan religion of the empire until Christianity was recognized under the Emperor Constantine (reign A.D. 305–337).

the lowest persons in the tax-collecting system from among the natives of the country. The taxpayers' hatred would be turned against these "traitors," and not against the Romans themselves. (See section on Matthew in chapter 7, "The Apostles.")

The people of Judea had to pay three major taxes. The first was the tax on the land, the *tributum soli*. The second was the *vectiqalia*, a general tax of the empire that included tax on imported goods at ports. Matthew probably collected this tax from returning fishermen at Capernaum, a town on the northwest shore of the Sea of Galilee. Last was the head tax, *tributum capitis*, the "tribute" we read of in the Gospels. Augustus started this tax and Quirinius, governor of Syria, attempted to carry it out. He ordered all natives of Judea to return to the town of their family to be counted for the new tax. Thus Mary and Joseph traveled to Bethlehem (Luke 2:1-3) at the time Jesus was born.

The tax issue continued to be a sore spot with the Jews and many small groups attempted revolt. During Jesus' ministry, taxes were still a serious matter (Matt. 17:24-27; Mark 12:13-17; Luke 20:21-26).

Quirinius' last act as governor was to install a new high priest, Annas (Luke 3:2; John 18:13, 24). Annas took office in A.D. 7 and was forced to resign after Augustus' death in A.D. 14.

Augustus' son-in-law, Tiberius (A.D. 14–37), became emperor after Augustus' death. He appointed Gratus as new governor of Judea. Gratus chose a number of high priests before selecting Caiaphas in about A.D. 18. Caiaphas held office until A.D. 36. During this time, he found Jesus guilty of blasphemy and sent him to Pilate for sentencing (Matt. 26:3, 57; Luke 18:13-14, 24, 28).

Pontius Pilate had replaced Valerius Gratus as governor in A.D. 26. He had gotten off to a bad start by ordering the legion of soldiers in the fortress of Antonia to carry a bust of the emperor Tiberius as its emblem. The Jews considered this emblem to be an idol; they rebelled when the soldiers paraded it through the streets during the Day of Atonement.

The trial of Jesus in about A.D. 32 was another in a long series of skirmishes between Pilate and the Jews. Pilate feared that if he were lenient with Jesus, the Jews would stage another uprising, so he had Jesus crucified (Matt. 27:11-26; Mark 15:1-15; Luke 23:1-25; John 18:28-19:16). Pilate was removed from office in A.D. 36, when he reacted too strongly to a meeting of Samaritans on Mount Gerizim. Pilate's journey to Rome for punishment was stopped when Tiberius died in A.D. 37.

Tiberius and his successors—Caligula, Claudius, and Nero—were known as the Julio-Claudian emperors. Caligula (A.D. 37–41) was a madman who once installed a horse as an official in his government. Being convinced of his own divinity, he ordered a statue of himself to be placed in the Jerusalem temple. He was assassinated before this command could be executed.

At the beginning of his reign (A.D. 41–54), Claudius (cf. Acts 11:28; 18:2) tried to suppress the anti-Jewish activities that Caligula had begun. But later he turned against the Jews. Suetonius says Claudius "expelled from Rome the Jews, who were constantly rioting under the leadership of Chrestus."

The immoral behavior of Nero (A.D. 54–68) is well-known. He ordered his wife and mother killed, and persecuted Christians during his rule. Nero's rumored resurrection may be symbolically mentioned in Revelation 13:3.

Vespasian took the imperial throne in A.D. 69. He had served as commander of the Syrian frontier army when the final fight between Romans and Jews began to surface in A.D. 66. In the summer of that year, Jewish terrorists slaughtered the Roman troops at Masada and prepared for a strong defense. The leader of the temple in Jerusalem stopped the daily offerings for the emperor's well-being. Vespasian was given the task of subduing the Jewish revolt. By the summer of A.D. 68, Jerusalem was near defeat and Vespasian was made emperor. He allowed his son Titus to make the final assault. In A.D. 70, Jerusalem was destroyed. Herod's temple was burned

Arch of Titus. Emperor Titus of Rome (rule A.D. 79–81) built this imposing monument to commemorate his victories. Among the scenes depicted on the arch is the Romans' looting of the temple at Jerusalem. (A.D. 70). Titus was the commander of the Roman army at that time.

and its sacred furniture carried off to Rome. The remaining Jewish guerillas were defeated during the next two years. By A.D. 73, all traces of a self-ruling Jewish nation were erased.

ROME'S CONTRIBUTIONS

The Romans were not very original in their abstract thinking, but they were quick to adapt good ideas from people they conquered. For instance, the Romans took the simple Doric columns of Greek architecture and turned them into the more ornate Corinthian style. The remains of Roman roads, walls, bridges, amphitheaters, and basilicas still impress tourists today.

The Romans held law and order above all other things. They treated conquered people with justice and tact. The Romans instituted the three branches of government—legislative, executive, and judicial—that became the basis for American democracy. Many aspects of Roman law survive in modern governments around the world.

The Latin language flowered in the first century B.C., giving us classic poetry and prose. Pliny the Elder and other Latin writers recorded excellent histories of the empire. For centuries, Latin influenced the languages and literature in Europe. English words such as *citizen, census, senate,* and *fiscal* survive from Roman days.

The Romans had little use for a complex religion; they invoked gods only to help their family or state. Their chief gods were Jupiter, who controlled the universe; Mars, god of war; Juno, patron goddess of women; and Minerva, goddess of war, wisdom, and skill.

The Romans found a way to build concrete domes that allowed them to enclose large areas. They created what were probably the first hospital and medical schools. Many of the Romans' contributions still affect Western life today. The Roman world order was the greatest single influence upon the life of the Jews in the New Testament era.

5
THE JEWS IN NEW TESTAMENT TIMES

By the time of Jesus, Judaism had become a sectarian religion. Jews holding different beliefs spent many hours arguing difficult questions of law, history, and politics. They debated questions such as, "Who is a true Jew?" "What does God require of His People?" and "What is the destiny of Israel?" Their conflicting answers revealed sharp differences between the various Jewish sects of New Testament times.

OLD TESTAMENT BACKGROUND

As we review the history of the Old Testament, we find many factors that contributed to the hostility between the Jewish parties of Jesus' day.

A. Differences among the Twelve Tribes. Many centuries had blurred the individual characteristics of Jacob's twelve sons (cf. Gen. 49). Nevertheless, the nation that grew out of 12 brothers inevitably preserved some of their characteristics. Sectarian divisions often followed family lines as descendants of the 12 brothers continued their bitter rivalry.

People in Jesus' day were interested in tracing their lineage for at least four reasons: to establish covenantal rights to position or property, to identify themselves with the promised Messiah, to identify themselves with well-known priests, or simply to establish their family "roots."

Knowing one's family origin provided a certain amount of comfort and stability in the troubled times of the first century. No doubt this is why many Jews were careful to preserve a record of their family tree. They were proud to identify themselves with a Jewish tribe that had a long and noble heritage. Even Paul boasted of his Jewish family background (2 Cor. 11:22; Phil. 3:5-6). Nation, tribe, breeding, and place of birth—these were the standards that first-century Jews used to evaluate themselves.

B. The Exile: God Turns His Back. To fully appreciate the character of each Jewish sect, we must review the events that took place in Israel after the Exile. In 734 B.C. the Assyrian king Tiglath-Pileser III sent the first Israelites into exile. This was the first of a series of deportations that continued through A.D. 70. The Jews were scattered throughout the known world, where they became known as the *Diaspora* (Greek, "scattering").

In 723 B.C. the Assyrians deported another group of Israelites from the Promised Land, sending Assyrian colonists to take their place. The Babylonians conquered the southern kingdom of Judea in 597 B.C. When Jewish leaders in Palestine rebelled against their Babylonian overlords, the Babylonians attacked the southern kingdom again in 586 B.C. and 581 B.C. After the last attack, they sent more than 70,000 Jews into exile.

The Exile had profound and lasting effects on Israel. Jews of the *Diaspora* were tempted to eat "non-kosher" foods (Dan. 1:5, 8) and break other ceremonial laws. Their captors sometimes required them to worship idols (Dan. 3:4-7). As the Captivity continued, more Jews defected from the faith of their ancestors. This created tension between Jews who adopted pagan life-styles and those who did not, and it caused the Jews to split into various factions after the Exile. Some Jewish leaders felt that the returning Jews should renounce their pagan ways (cf. Ezra 9–10) while others believed they should relax some requirements of the Law.

During the Exile many Jews became confused and skeptical. The Hebrew language was dying off, and with it those who cared for the Torah. The temple had been destroyed and animal sacrifices stopped. No longer was it clear what God required of His people.

C. Jewish Mysticism. Elements of pagan religion began to fill the voids created by skepticism and doubt. Some Jews "hedged" their faith by dabbling in astrology and the occult. They moved into these areas very slowly, and Jewish leaders did not realize at first what was happening. But Jewish mystics began to reinterpret the traditional Jewish teachings in light of the pagan beliefs they had accepted.

For example, Jews of the *Diaspora* became fascinated with demons and angels. They qualified the biblical belief in a Creator who has sovereign control of His creation, by adopting a Persian view of the universe with an elaborate spirit world and an ongoing war between the forces of light and of darkness.

Jewish mystics compiled these beliefs in groups of religious writings known as the *deuterocanon* and *pseudepigrapha.* Some deuterocanonical books, such as the Book of Tobit, promoted astrology and the teachings of Zoroastrianism, which came from Persia. The story of Tobit asserts the victory of God over pagan demons—but in the process it acknowledges the power of pagan demons. Moreover, it portrays God as a great force behind the events of life, rather than a personal presence in the midst of His people. This erosion of the Jewish faith made it more difficult for the Jews to believe that Jesus was "Immanuel . . . God with us" (cf. Matt. 1:23). Many Jews still held to the pagan belief that God had removed himself from man's everyday life.

D. The Orthodox Response. Not all Jews succumbed to pagan beliefs during the Exile. Many Jewish leaders realized that these ideas threatened the survival of the Torah. Without the Law, the Jews would have no hope. Religious compromise would lead them farther and farther away from God's Word, until they were lost among the surrounding cultures.

Jewish leaders responded to this threat by establishing synagogues, instituting the office of rabbi, and emphasizing the need for a faithful "remnant." These changes guaranteed the survival of Judaism, but they also helped to create new factions among the Jews.

1. The Synagogue. The Greek word *synagogue* means "a gathering together." It denotes the gathering of *Diaspora* Jews for worship and study outside the temple. The Old Testament does not mention synagogue worship; but Philo, Josephus, and the Midrash claimed that Moses began this institution in the wilderness. More likely the exiled Jews created the synagogue when they came together to pray, sing songs, and discuss the Torah as they lived in foreign lands. After they returned from the Exile, they made the synagogue a formal institution.

When the Babylonians destroyed the temple in Jerusalem and ended the Jewish system of animal sacrifice, Jews came to understand that prayer was the "sacrifice of the heart." They made prayer the central act of synagogue worship.

Perhaps Ezra inaugurated synagogue worship in Israel when he called the great assembly in Jerusalem (Neh. 8). The activities of the assembly closely paralleled those of the synagogues including the gathering of the "chiefs of the fathers of all the people" for Torah study (Neh. 8:13).

It is doubtful that the Jews ever intended to replace the temple with the synagogue. But their experience in exile made them realize that they could be faithful to God without worshiping at the temple. It was easy to form a synagogue; only 10 Jewish men were needed. And the synagogue was a natural environment for theological training.

As long as the restored temple stood in Jerusalem, synagogue worship played a secondary role in Jewish life. Even so, archaeologists have found the remains of at least 50 synagogues outside Palestine—11 of them in Rome. The Book of Acts identifies synagogues in 8 cities of Asia Minor (Acts 9:2, 20; 3:5, 15; 14:1; 17:1, 10; 18:4, 26; 26; 19:8).

Synagogues promoted the growth of Jewish sects. Special-interest groups could use a synagogue as a platform for voicing their opinions when they disagreed with the leaders of the temple or the nation.

2. The Rabbinate. Each synagogue had a few members who were exceptionally well-versed in the Torah. Because of this, they were allowed to expound their views to the synagogue community. The Jews called such a leader a *rabbi* (Hebrew, "teacher").

Each synagogue had its own standards for choosing rabbis,

Star of David. This six-pointed star is widely used as a symbol of Judaism. The history of its origin is lost, but it decorated Jewish architecture by the third century A.D. Later called the "seal of Solomon," the symbol was apparently first mentioned in Jewish literature of the fourteenth century A.D. It seems that this symbol was not used in biblical times.

so the quality of rabbinic teaching was unpredictable. After the Jews came under the influence of Hellenistic thought, they began to organize and record the teachings of various rabbis.

One of these collections was called the *Mishna* (Hebrew, "repetition"). It contained the legal opinions of respected rabbis, which had been handed down orally for many generations. The Mishna sometimes cited the Torah in support of a rabbi's position, but it did not attempt to analyze the Scripture itself. Jewish scholars believe that the first Mishna was compiled around 5 B.C.

An older collection of rabbinic tradition was called the *Midrash* (Hebrew, "commentary"). The Midrash contained the rabbis' interpretation of Scripture. The *Soferim* (scribes) compiled the first Midrash in the fourth century B.C. Because the Midrash was older than the Mishna and was directly tied to Scripture, first-century Jews relied upon it more heavily than the Mishna. However, the Jewish sects preferred to use their own rabbis' Mishna, since it elevated their group's ideas to the status of holy writ.

After the Exile, the Persians used Jewish scribes to enforce civil laws in Palestine. This created conflicting loyalties among the Jewish leaders, who found that they had to align themselves with the political "power brokers" in order to survive. This pattern continued into the Roman era.

Jesus and Paul understood the conflicts that the rabbinic system produced. Jesus told His disciples not to be called "rabbi" (Matt. 23:8) and Paul admonished the Corinthians to stop lining up behind their favorite teacher (1 Cor. 3:3-9).

3. Remnant Theology. Mainline Jews also combated the drift toward paganism by stressing *remnant theology*. In other words, they declared that God would preserve a faithful remnant of His people who would be the seed of a new Israel. For the first time, they entertained the notion that not all Jews were the chosen of God. To be a true Israelite, a person had to obey the Law of Moses.

From the very beginning, God had revealed that His people must obey Him. History proved that any of Abraham's descendants who rebelled against God failed to receive His blessing (e.g., Esau and Ishmael). So God had always required obedience. But the Exile drove the point home.

More than one group considered itself to be the faithful remnant of God's people. Remnant theology spawned several secret cults with mysterious worship rituals, designed to set them apart from the corrupt majority of Jews.

When Cyrus the Great allowed the Jews to return to Palestine, he confronted them with a choice: Would they go back to the Promised Land or would they be content to live in the lands of exile? The Jews who chose to return believed those who stayed behind were less faithful. They considered themselves to be the faithful remnant God would use to establish His kingdom on earth.

HELLENISM AND THE JEWS

The armies of Alexander the Great introduced another factor that divided the Jews—the cultural influence of Hellenism.

Alexander promoted Greek culture in every land that he conquered. When his armies took Palestine from the Persians in 332 B.C., they required the Jews to adopt the language and customs of Greece. *(See* chapter 3, "The Greeks and Hellenism.")* Jewish scholars began reading Greek philosophy in the libraries of Alexandria and other cities Alexander built along his line of march. They were intrigued by the ideas of Aristotle and other Greek thinkers, especially when they saw the success of Alexander's Greek-based civilization.

The Greek philosophers wanted logical answers to the questions of life. They dared to think in abstract concepts

Synagogue school. During the Babylonian Exile, Jews were unable to sacrifice because they lived in an unclean land far from the temple. Their need for a worship community led to the establishment of the synagogue, a place for reading and studying the Old Testament. Jewish boys learned the Law from their *rabbi,* or teacher, in a synagogue school.

instead of dealing only with physical objects. Jewish scholars embraced these methods, falling under the persuasion that Greek logic would help them untangle the complex traditions of the rabbis.

After Alexander died in 323 B.C., his generals carved up the empire he had won. Ptolemy I established a dynasty in Alexandria. He captured Jerusalem and brought Jewish captives to colonize the area around his capital city in Egypt. Ptolemy made them full citizens in his new empire and invited Jewish scholars to use the famous libraries of Alexandria. His successor, Ptolemy II, commissioned a Greek translation of the Old Testament for the library; this translation came to be known as the *Septuagint*. Jews of New Testament times used the Septuagint in place of the Hebrew manuscripts, since Greek had become their common language.

Alexandria produced several Jewish scholars who brought Hellenistic ideas into their writings. The most famous of these was Philo (*ca.* 20 B.C.–A.D. 50). Philo believed that the Scriptures contained the highest truth available to mankind; but he also believed that the Greek philosophies supplied important facets of truth that complemented the Scriptures.

Another of Alexander's generals, Seleucus I, established a dynasty in Syria. He eventually pushed the Ptolemies out of Palestine. But the Seleucids gradually lost control of the Palestinian frontier until the Seleucid king Antiochus III was defeated by the Romans at the Battle of Magnesia in 190 B.C. The Romans made the Seleucid Empire a satellite of their own growing empire. Because of their Greek background, the Seleucids continued to impose a Greek way of life upon their Jewish subjects.

Antiochus IV had to pay heavy tribute to the Roman Emperor. To raise this money, he decided to sell the office of Jewish high priest. First he gave it to Jason, a brother of the high priest Onias III (2 Macc. 4:7-17). Two years later, Jason's friend Menelaus offered to pay 300 talents more for the office; Antiochus deposed Jason and put Menelaus in his place (2 Macc. 4:23). Menelaus ignored the Jewish laws, building a gymnasium in Jerusalem where naked athletes met for Greek sporting contests. In fact, Menelaus and his friends "hid their circumcision" (1 Macc. 1:14-15), probably by surgical methods, so they would look like Greeks when they entered the public baths. Apparently many Hellenistic Jews were embarrassed by their circumcision, for it later became an issue in the church at Corinth (1 Cor. 7:18).

After he installed Menelaus as high priest, Antiochus went on a rampage. He confiscated the property of Jerusalem's citizens and ransacked the temple to fill his treasury. Then he set up a pagan altar in the temple, where he sacrificed a pig— an outright violation of Mosaic Law. Antiochus ordered his subjects to build Greek altars in all the villages of Palestine. He outlawed the Mosaic rituals, punishing those who attempted to observe them (1 Macc. 1:29-62).

A. The Maccabeans. The insults of Antiochus IV enraged the Jews of Palestine. In 166 B.C. a group of Jewish rebels gathered around Mattathias and his five sons in the village of Modein, a few miles northwest of Jerusalem. They began a series of attacks on Antiochus and his successors. Historians call this conflict the Maccabean Wars, after Mattathias' son Judas Maccabeus. The Jewish guerillas fought their Hellenistic rulers from 166 to 143 B.C. Mattathias called for everyone who was "zealous for the law, and maintained the covenant" (1 Macc. 2:27) to join the struggle. We are not sure how many Jews cast in their lot with the Maccabeans, but the rebels seemed to have broad popular support. We are told that Antiochus' army massacred 1,000 Jewish warriors because they refused to fight on the Sabbath (1 Macc. 2:29-38). This disaster caused the Maccabeans to relax their observance of the Sabbath, at least for the duration of the war.

Josephus and other historians of the time note that a group called a *Hasidim* joined forces with the Maccabeans. The *Hasidim* were "mighty men of Israel, even all such as were voluntary devoted unto the law" (1 Macc. 2:42). Apparently the *Hasidim* (Hebrew, "holy ones") piously devoted themselves to observing the Law of Moses. They wanted the right to obey this Law in their native land once again. But they were not interested in reestablishing a Jewish political state to achieve this. In 163 B.C., Judas Maccabeus persuaded King Demetrius to give the Jews religious freedom once again, and the *Hasidim* soon stopped fighting. But the new high priest, Alcimus, ordered the execution of 60 *Hasidim* to retaliate for the success of the Maccabeans. This caused the *Hasidim* to take up arms once again (1 Macc. 7:13-20).

As the Maccabean Wars dragged on, the Jewish rebels were able to regain more and more of Palestine. Judas' successor, Jonathan, made a new treaty with Rome to assure that the Romans would intervene if the Syrians launched an all-out war against the Jews. At last the Maccabeans controlled most of the Promised Land, and they named their leader Simon "governor and high priest forever until there should arise a faithful prophet" (1 Macc. 14:25-49). By doing this, they established Simon's family as a new line of priests.

B. The Hasmoneans. Simon's descendants were known as the "house of Hasmon," or Hasmoneans. Simon's third son, John Hyrcanus, named himself king and high priest in 135 B.C. Thus he began a new Jewish dynasty that would last until the Romans invaded Palestine.

Antiochus IV died in a campaign against the Romans in 128 B.C. This gave the Jews a free hand to govern themselves in Palestine. They revived the sacrificial system established by the Law of Moses, hoping to bring a new golden age to Israel. But the Torah (written Law) was not directly the standard for the new Jewish state. Instead the people followed oral traditions, received from rabbis who had taught their ancestors during the Exile. Over 600 years, Jews of the *Diaspora* had developed many different interpretations of the Law, suited to the situations in which they lived. In Palestine, these conflicting ideas now faced each other head-on. This set the stage for New Testament Judaism.

The Roman general Pompey invaded Palestine in 63 B.C. *(See* "The Romans.") He captured the city of Jerusalem and forced the Hasmoneans to become puppet rulers for Rome. The Hasmoneans continued to serve in this capacity until 47 B.C., when the Romans allowed Antipater to take control of

Judea's government. Antipater divided the offices of priest and king, making himself the first ruler in a line of kings known as the Herodians.

JEWISH SECTS IN NEW TESTAMENT TIMES

When Jesus was born, the Jews of Palestine were divided into three major factions: Pharisees, Sadducees, and Essenes. Within each of these Jewish parties, small groups of Jews rallied around the teachings of a particular rabbi or his rabbinic school. So when we discuss the three major parties of New Testament Judaism, we should remember that the Jews of each group had a broad range of views.

A. Pharisees: Law Experts. During the time of John Hyrcanus, the *Pharisees* emerged from the old party of the *Hasidim*. The Pharisees were the master interpreters of the oral traditions of the rabbis. Most of them came from middle-class families of artisans and tradesmen (e.g., the apostle Paul was a tentmaker). They exerted a powerful influence over the peasant masses. Josephus observed that when the Jewish people faced an important decision, they relied on the opinion of the Pharisees rather than that of the king or high priest *(Antiquities,* Bk. XII, Chap. X, Sect. 5). Because the people trusted them, the Pharisees were chosen for high government positions, including the Sanhedrin. Josephus estimates that only 6,000 Pharisees lived in Palestine during the time of Jesus, so they needed popular support. Perhaps this is why they feared Jesus' ability to attract great crowds.

The Pharisees taught that righteous people would live again after death (Acts 23:8), while the wicked would be punished for eternity. Not many other Jewish groups accepted this view. Instead they espoused the Greek and Persian idea that death permanently separated the soul from the body.

This may also help to explain why the crowds followed Jesus. He was a poor carpenter, yet a master teacher of the Law (Matt. 7:28-29); moreover, He taught that the dead would live again (Luke 14:14; John 11:25). Jesus' teachings about a person's diet (Mark 7:1-9), respect for elders (Mark 7:10-13), and Sabbath keeping (Matt. 12:24-32) agreed with the teachings of the Pharisees. Also, He often spoke of angels, demons, and other spirits such as Jewish mystics had described. This attracted the interest of the common people.

B. Sadducees: Guardians of the Torah. After the Maccabeans drove the Syrians out of Palestine, the Hellenistic Jews went into hiding. It was no longer safe for a Jewish scholar to endorse Greek ideas. Yet these Jewish intellectuals continued to apply their logic to the problems of the day, and they formed a new Jewish sect known as the *Sadducees.*

We are not sure what the name *Sadducee* originally meant. Most scholars believe it was derived from the Hebrew word

The Sanhedrin. During most of the Roman period, the internal government of Judea was controlled by the Sanhedrin, the highest tribunal of the Jews. The Sanhedrin, a group of elders, presided over by the high priest, could mete out capital punishment until about forty years before the destruction of Jerusalem. After that time, it could not execute the sentence of death without the confirmation of the Roman procurator, which is why Jesus had to be tried before Pilate (John 18:31-32).

saddig ("righteous") or that it comes from the priestly name Zadok, since the Sadducees were connected with the temple priesthood.

The Sadducees rejected the oral tradition of the rabbis. They accepted only the written Law of Moses, and condemned any teaching that was not based on the written Word (Josephus, *Antiquities,* Bk. XIII, Chap. X, Sect. 6). They saw too many Persian and Assyrian influences in the teachings of the Pharisees, and felt the Pharisees were traitors to the Jewish tradition. They rejected the Pharisaic belief in angels, demons, and resurrection after death (Matt. 22:23-32; Acts 23:8). Thus they opposed Jesus when he agreed with the Pharisees (Matt. 22:31-32).

The Sadducees adopted the beliefs of the Greek philosopher Epicurus, who said that the soul dies with the body (Josephus, *Antiquities,* Bk. XVIII, Chap. II, Sect. 4). They taught that each person is the master of his own fate.

The Sadducees loved to debate matters of theology and philosophy—another clue to their Greek interests. Their sophisticated ideas did not appeal to the masses, so in politics they had to join hands with the Pharisees. In fact, the Sadducees might have disappeared from the scene before New Testament times, had it not been for a strange twist of events in Jewish politics:

The Pharisees opposed John Hyrcanus' decision to become high priest, because they heard that Hyrcanus' mother had been raped during the reign of terror of Antiochus IV. Hyrcanus proved that the story was a lie, but the Pharisaic court punished the liar with only a few lashings. This angered Hyrcanus, who threw his support to the Sadducees.

Hyrcanus' son, Alexander Janneus (104–78 B.C.), had studied under Greek tutors in Rome. He was sympathetic to Greek ideas and secretly favored the intellectual Sadducees. Josephus reports that Janneus became drunk at the Feast of Tabernacles one year and poured an offering of water at his own feet, instead of on the altar. (Perhaps this was Janneus' way of showing his contempt for the Pharisees, who poured water on the altar to symbolize the need for rain.) A riot broke

out, Janneus' soldiers restored order, but only after 6,000
people had been killed (Josephus, *Antiquities,* Bk. XIII, Chap.
V, Sect. 13). The Pharisees waged a bitter civil war against
Janneus (94–88 B.C.), which the Hasmonean king ended by
crucifying the Pharisaic leaders and 800 of their followers.

Hyrcanus' wife Salome had a more tolerant attitude toward
the Pharisees during her reign (78–69 B.C.). But the Pharisees
and Sadducees never forgot this bloody episode.

C. Essenes: Righteous Radicals. The Essenes also
emerged from the pious movement known as the *Hasidim.*
Josephus tells us there were two groups of Essenes (*War,* Bk.
II, Chap. VIII, Sect. 2), while the third-century bishop
Hippolytus says there were four groups of Essenes (cf. his
Refutation of All Heresies). There may have been even more.

The name *Essene* comes from a Hebrew word that means
"pious" or "holy." Although other Jews called them by this
name, Essenes themselves probably rejected the label. They
did not consider themselves to be especially holy or pious; but
they saw themselves as the guardians of mysterious truths that
would govern the life of Israel when the Messiah appeared.

Most scholars believe the Zadokite Documents, found in a
Cairo synagogue around 1896, were written by an Essene
group. These manuscripts describe the final battle between
Good and Evil that would prepare the way for the Messiah.

The Essenes planned to keep this type of information a
secret until the proper time. They probably identified themselves with the *maskilim,* or "they that understand," who the
prophet Daniel said would guide the Jews in their time of
turmoil (Dan. 11:33; 12:9-10).

Most of the Essenes lived in communities in remote desert
areas. Others lived in a quarter of Jerusalem and there was
even an Essenes' Gate. They practiced elaborate rites to purify
themselves, physically and spiritually. Their writings (that is,
the Dead Sea Scrolls, which most scholars regard as Essene)
show that they were very careful to avoid being corrupted by
the society around them, in the hope that God would honor
their faithfulness. They called their leader the Teacher of
Righteousness.

The Jewish Colony at Elephantine

"In that day shall there be an altar to the Lord in the midst of the land of Egypt, and a pillar at the border thereof to the Lord" (Isa. 19:19). This prophecy was fulfilled, at least in part, when soldiers under the banner of King Ashurbanipal of Assyria stormed into Egypt in 663 B.C. Among the Assyrian troops were hundreds of Jewish mercenaries—soldiers known for their bravery and for their allegiance to the living God.

These men enjoyed most of the freedoms of civilian life. They married, raised families, and entered into local politics and business. In time, some of them became prominent businessmen, involved in the ivory trade that gave Elephantine its name.

Their ranks were swollen in 587 B.C., when Nebuchadnezzar laid waste to Jerusalem after a revolt there and carried her inhabitants off to exile. Many Jews fled into Egypt during this tragic period, and a number of them were happy to find a thriving Jewish community awaiting them at Elephantine. By this time, there was even a magnificent temple in the island city.

The temple had been built some time around the year 600 at great expense. It was an impressive edifice that included huge stone pillars and five gates with bronze hinges. Inside, silver and golden bowls were stored. These were to be used only in the worship of Yahweh.

Although Yahweh continued to be supreme in the worship of the Egyptian Jews, He came to be regarded as one of many gods. Ultimately, they believed that goddesses Eshem-bethel and Anath-bethel shared the temple with Him. Presumably, these were considered to be His wives; their introduction into the worship probably grew out of the Jews' own intermarriage with the local population.

The temple at Elephantine was destroyed in 410 B.C. by priests of the god Khnum. The Jews appealed to Jerusalem for help with rebuilding, but were surprised by the rebuke they received. The priests in Jerusalem regarded the existence of a second temple as close to blasphemy. Despite the absence of a temple, the Jewish community at Elephantine thrived until shortly after the time of Christ. With the spreading of Christianity, it simply faded out of the picture. The present city of Aswan was built largely with materials taken from the site of Elephantine.

It is interesting to note that women at Elephantine enjoyed greater status than anywhere else in the Hebrew world. They were able to divorce their husbands, for instance, and could refuse to marry someone. These practices were unheard of in most of Jewish society of that day.

Archaeologists have uncovered dozens of papyrus manuscripts at Elephantine, which are valuable indicators of the changes in Hebrew writing during the intertestamental period. The manuscripts show that Jewish writers were strongly influenced by Aramaic and (later) Greek scribal techniques.

The Dead Sea Scrolls do not identify the people who lived in the Qumran community, where the scrolls were written; but the Roman historian Pliny said this area was the headquarters of the Essene sect. In 1947 a Bedouin shepherd boy cast a stone into a cave at Khirbet Qumran (on the northwest coast of the Dead Sea) and heard the breaking of a clay jar. The boy entered the cave and found several jars containing ancient manuscripts. Scholars identified them as the Book of Isaiah, a commentary on Habakkuk, and several documents that con-

The Herods

The family of the Herods exerted Rome's control over Palestine during the time of Christ and the founding of the Christian church. This family ruled tyrannically—and often violently—for about one hundred years.

The family that became known as the Herods were Idumean by birth. (Idumea was an area south of Bethlehem and Jerusalem, populated by the Edomites—former Jews who had refused to "inhabit the land" of Canaan.) The Maccabean leader John Hyrcanus I had conquered the Idumeans in about 126 B.C. and compelled them to accept orthodox Judaism. The Herod family ruled Idumea when the Maccabean dynasty began to lose control of Palestine.

The Maccabean family had led the Jews in a heroic struggle to free themselves from foreign rule. However, political intrigue and family jealousy among the Maccabeans left the Jewish state in a weakened condition, making it a prey to Rome. The last strong ruler of the Maccabean (later called the Hasmonean) line was Alexander Jannaeus. When he died (*ca.* 78 B.C.), he left

the kingdom to his widow, Alexandra Salome. She made her older son, John Hyrcanus II, high priest and hoped to groom him for the throne. But Alexandra suddenly became ill and died, and her younger son Aristobulus proclaimed himself king. The Herods took advantage of this confused situation.

Antipater I of Idumea, father of Herod the Great, was cunning, wealthy, and ambitious. He allied himself with John Hyrcanus II in a bid to overthrow Aristobulus. They drew the Romans into the struggle and won. Antipater reinstated Hyrcanus II as high priest, and Julius Caesar later appointed Antipater as governor of Judea.

Antipater gave two of his sons positions in the government—Phasael was made prefect of Jerusalem and Herod was governor of Galilee. Herod ("the Great") was intelligent, charming in manners, and quite capable in statecraft. Like his father he was highly ambitious. But the Sanhedrin (Jewish legal council) turned against the young ruler when he executed some Jews without official consent; in fact, they demanded his

---

tained the teachings of the Qumran sect. Eventually they found 11 caves with ancient scrolls and fragments. The caves yielded fragments or copies of every book of the Old Testament except Esther. Most of the manuscripts had been written in the time of the Maccabees. This discovery sparked archaeologists' interest in the ruins of Khirbet Qumran itself, where they found a large room for copying manuscripts.

Scholars still debate whether the people of Qumran were actually Essenes, since their writings disagree with known Essene teachings at several points. Some believe that Pharisees who fled from the rage of Janneus (88 B.C.) settled at Qumran. (A commentary on the Book of Nahum found at Qumran seems to refer to the life-style of the Pharisees.) But if the people of Qumran were simply another splintered Essene group, that would account for their occasional departures from the mainstream of Essene teachings.

death. He appealed to the Roman governor of Syria, who dismissed the Jews' charges and extended Herod's governorship to Coele-Syria and Samaria.

When Cassius, one of Julius Caesar's murderers, became ruler of the eastern sector of the Roman Empire, Herod and his father Antipater gave him their full cooperation. Many Jewish groups opposed their rule, and Antipater died of poisoning in 43 B.C. just after he paid a large tax to Cassius.

Then Mark Antony assumed control of the eastern provinces, and Jewish leaders clamored to denounce Herod as a tyrant. But Antony confirmed Herod and Phasael *tetrarchs* (i.e., each was ruler of one fourth of the region) of Judea.

In 40 B.C., the Hasmonean leader Antigonus (a nephew of John Hyrcanus I) ousted Herod from power and was proclaimed king of Judea. He ordered his men to cut off the ears of Hyrcanus II, so that he could no longer be high priest. (It was unlawful for a mutilated person to serve as priest.) Herod appealed to Antony for aid. Octavian and Antony advised the Roman

senate to appoint Herod king of the Jews, but it took him three years of hard fighting to regain his kingdom. From that time until his death 33 years later, Herod governed his realm as a loyal ally of Rome.

When Octavian defeated Antony and Cleopatra at Actium in 31 B.C., Herod wisely surrendered his kingdom to his new master. Octavian confirmed Herod as king of Judea and added still more territory to his domain.

Herod the Great married a total of ten women—Doris, Mariamne I, Mariamne II, Malthace, Cleopatra, Pallas, Phaedra, Elpis, and two whose names are unknown (in that order). In all, they bore him at least fifteen children.

Herod divorced Doris in order to marry Mariamne (known historically as Mariamne I). She was a member of the Hasmonean family, and Herod hoped to gain political status through this marriage. Eventually, Herod ordered his men to execute Mariamne I and her grandfather John Hyrcanus II. By doing this, Herod exterminated the Hasmonean family.

(Continued on page 104)

D. Zealots. Pompey's invasion of Palestine in 63 B.C. destroyed the Jews' hopes of restoring their own government. But some groups stubbornly insisted that the Jews must repel the Roman invaders. These "Zealots" tried to stir up rebellion among the Jews.

The best-known Zealot leader was Judas the Galilean (Acts 5:37). When Augustus decreed that "all the world should be taxed" (Luke 2:2), Judas led an ill-fated revolt against the Romans. Josephus observed that this was the beginning of the Jews' conflicts with the Roman Empire, which ended with the destruction of the temple in A.D. 70 (*Antiquities,* Bk. VIII, Chap. VIII).

Judas and his followers resented any foreign control of their government. Their thinking probably inspired the question that one Pharisee put to Jesus, "Is it lawful to pay taxes to Caesar?" (Mark 12:14).

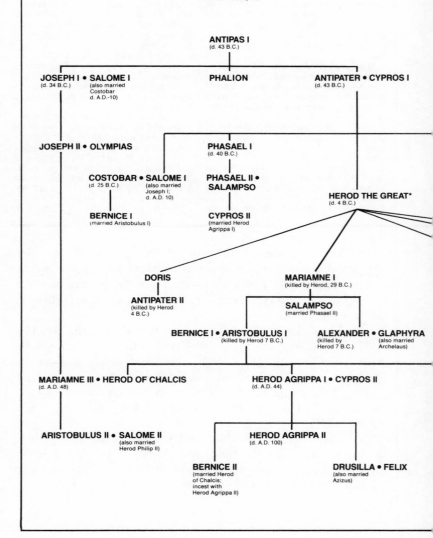

THE HERODS' FAMILY TREE
(simplified)

Ⓒ Thomas Nelson, Inc.

ANTIPAS I
(d. 43 B.C.)

JOSEPH I • **SALOME I**
(d. 34 B.C.) (also married Costobar d. A.D.-10)

PHALION

ANTIPATER • **CYPROS I**
(d. 43 B.C.)

JOSEPH II • **OLYMPIAS**

PHASAEL I
(d. 40 B.C.)

COSTOBAR • **SALOME I**
(d. 25 B.C.) (also married Joseph I; d. A.D. 10)

PHASAEL II • **SALAMPSO**

BERNICE I
(married Aristobulus I)

CYPROS II
(married Herod Agrippa I)

HEROD THE GREAT*
(d. 4 B.C.)

DORIS

MARIAMNE I
(killed by Herod, 29 B.C.)

ANTIPATER II
(killed by Herod 4 B.C.)

SALAMPSO
(married Phasael II)

BERNICE I • **ARISTOBULUS I**
(killed by Herod 7 B.C.)

ALEXANDER • **GLAPHYRA**
(killed by Herod 7 B.C.) (also married Archelaus)

MARIAMNE III • **HEROD OF CHALCIS**
(d. A.D. 48)

HEROD AGRIPPA I • **CYPROS II**
(d. A.D. 44)

ARISTOBULUS II • **SALOME II**
(also married Herod Philip II)

HEROD AGRIPPA II
(d. A.D. 100)

BERNICE II
(married Herod of Chalcis; incest with Herod Agrippa II)

DRUSILLA • **FELIX**
(also married Azizus)

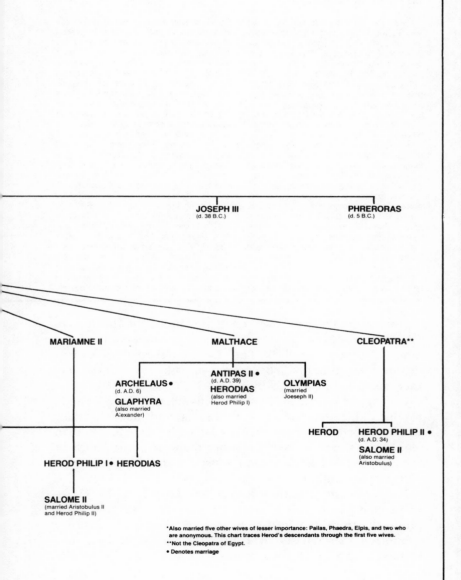

JOSEPH III
(d. 38 B.C.)

PHRERORAS
(d. 5 B.C.)

MARIAMNE II

MALTHACE

CLEOPATRA**

ARCHELAUS •
(d. A.D. 6)
GLAPHYRA
(also married
Alexander)

ANTIPAS II •
(d. A.D. 39)
HERODIAS
(also married
Herod Philip I)

OLYMPIAS
(married
Joeseph II)

HEROD

HEROD PHILIP II •
(d. A.D. 34)
SALOME II
(also married
Aristobulus)

HEROD PHILIP I • **HERODIAS**

SALOME II
(married Aristobulus II
and Herod Philip II)

*Also married five other wives of lesser importance: Pailas, Phaedra, Elpis, and two who
 are anonymous. This chart traces Herod's descendants through the first five wives.
**Not the Cleopatra of Egypt.
• Denotes marriage

The Herods (continued)

Herod the Great tried to win the Jews' favor by rebuilding their temple on a magnificent scale. Yet he also built temples dedicated to pagan gods. The Jewish people resented Herod's Idumean ancestry and his marriage to Malthace, a Samaritan.

The last years of Herod's life were dismal and full of grief; he deteriorated mentally and physically. His mad jealousy caused him to order many executions. Three of his sons—Antipater II, Alexander, and Aristobulus I—were among the victims.

Herod's death in 4 B.C. brought a new era to Judea. Just before his death, Herod formally gave the Roman emperor power to supervise his kingdom. (Rome had been the real ruler of Palestine since the overthrow of Aristobulus in 63 B.C., but it now exerted its control more directly.) In his will, Herod the Great divided his kingdom among three of his sons. Archelaus received Judea, Samaria, and Idumea; Antipas II received Galilee and Perea; and Herod Philip II received the northeastern territories.

Herod Archelaus ruled "in the room of his father Herod" (Matt. 2:22), although without

the title of king. He was Herod's oldest son by Malthace and had the worst reputation of all Herod's children. He angered the Jews by marrying Glaphyra, the widow of his half-brother Alexander. Rival Jews and Samaritans sent a united delegation to Rome, threatening to revolt if Archelaus were not removed. Accordingly, in A.D. 6, he was deposed and banished. Judea then became a Roman province, administered by governors appointed by the emperor.

Herod Antipas II was Herod's younger son by Malthace. The Gospels depict him as wholly immoral. He divorced his first wife to marry Herodias, the wife of his half-brother Herod Philip I; since Herodias was also his niece, their union was doubly sinful. He imprisoned John the Baptist for denouncing this marriage (Mark 6:17-18). Herodias made full use of her husband's pledge to give her daughter (possibly Salome II) anything that she wished (Mark 6:19-28). She demanded John's head on a platter, and so Antipas had him executed. However, Herod Antipas II was the ablest of Herod's sons; in A.D. 22 he built the city of Tiberias on the Sea of Galilee. Emperor

During the time Felix served as procurator of Judea (A.D. 52–60), the Zealots formed a radical group known as the *Sicarii* ("dagger people"). The *Sicarii* circulated in crowds during festivals and killed Roman sympathizers with daggers they concealed in their clothing.

During the war with Rome (A.D. 66–70), the *Sicarii* escaped to the old Jewish fortress at Masada and made it their headquarters. Two years after the fall of Jerusalem, a Roman legion laid siege to Masada. Rather than die at the hands of the Gentiles, the *Sicarii* killed themselves and their families— 960 people in all.

E. Herodians. Another Jewish sect known as the Herodians emerged during the Roman era. This was a political group that included Jews from various religious sects. They supported the dynasty of Herod the Great; in fact, they seemed to prefer Herod's oppressive home rule to the Ro-

Caligula exiled him in A.D. 39 after Herod Agrippa I accused him of plotting against Rome.

Herod Philip II was unlike the rest of the Herodian clan, for he was dignified, moderate, and just. He ruled for thirty-seven years as the "tetrarch of Iturea, and of the region of Trachonitis" (Luke 3:1). He married Salome II, the daughter of Herod Philip I, his half-brother.

Herod Agrippa I was the son of Aristobulus I and a grandson of Herod the Great. In A.D. 37, Emperor Caligula gave Agrippa the title of king, with territories northeast of Palestine. When Antipas II was banished in A.D. 39, Galilee and Perea were added to Agrippa's kingdom. Emperor Claudius further extended Agrippa's territory by giving him Judea and Samaria in A.D. 41. Agrippa I killed the apostle James and persecuted the early church. Because of his arrogance, God took his life (Acts 12). Among his children were Bernice II, Herod Agrippa II, and Drusilla (who married Felix, the Roman governor of Judea—cf. Acts 24:24).

Emperor Claudius gave Herod Agrippa II the title of king, with territories north and northeast of Palestine; these territories were increased by Emperor Nero in A.D. 56. His incestuous relationship with his sister Bernice II was a scandal among the Jews; the New Testament mentions that he and Bernice heard Paul (Acts 25:13–26:32). He urged his countrymen to remain loyal to Rome during the Jewish revolts; when the nation fell he moved to Rome, where he died in about A.D. 100.

Herod Philip I was Herod the Great's son by Mariamne II. For a time, he was included in Herod's will; but the king later revoked this grant. Philip remained a private citizen and his life story is unclear. His wife, Herodias, left him to live with his half-brother Antipas II (cf. Mark 6:17-18).

Christ, the apostles, and the early Christians lived during the turbulent days of the Herods. While the Herods built many splendid edifices and strengthened Judea militarily, the verdict of their subjects was that they were guilty—of oppression, tyranny, and burden in the highest degree.

man's foreign supervision. The Herodians are mentioned three times in the New Testament (Matt. 22:16; Mark 3:6; 12:13); but none of these passages gives us a clear picture of the Herodians' belief.

Some scholars believe Herodians thought Herod was the Messiah. But there is no hard evidence to support this view.

F. Samaritans. The Samaritans were descendants of the Jews who remained in Palestine after the Assyrians defeated Israel. They came from mixed marriages between Jews and Assyrian settlers who entered the Promised Land, so their very existence was a violation of God's Law. They worshiped God on Mount Gerizim, where they built their own temple and sacrificed animals. The Samaritans were despised by the Jews who returned from the Exile. They were called "that foolish people that dwell in Sichem [Shechem]" (Ecclesiasticus 50:25-26). In 128 B.C. John Hyrcanus destroyed the temple on

Tetradrachma of Bar-Kochba. After the fall of Jerusalem in A.D. 70, many groups of Jews continued to fight against the Romans, helping to regain their independence. Simon Bar-Kochba pronounced himself the Messiah and declared the independence of Judea. This Maccabean coin shows the facade of the temple and bears the legend *Simeon,* i.e., Simon (Bar-Kochba). He seized Jerusalem in A.D. 132, but the Romans retook the city and quashed the rebellion in A.D. 135. The land was desecrated and stripped; Jews were tortured, murdered, and sold as slaves on the open market; and the site of the temple was plowed under. From this time on, Jerusalem increasingly became a Gentile city.

Mount Gerizim. From this point on, Jews and Samaritans truly had no dealings with each other (cf. John 4:9).

In some ways, Jesus also stood aloof from the Samaritans. He told His disciples to stay away from the Gentiles and the cities of Samaria (Matt. 10:5-7). He brushed aside the Samaritan practice of worshiping only on Mount Gerizim (John 4:19-24). Yet Jesus was willing to visit a Samaritan village (Luke 9:52) and talk with a Samaritan woman (John 4:7-42), and His parable of the Good Samaritan suggests that in His view Samaritans might be more faithful to the Law than the Jews were (Luke 10:25-37). When Jesus healed ten lepers, a Samaritan man was the only one who returned to thank Him (Luke 17:11-19). And when Jesus commissioned His disciples to their mission of preaching the gospel, He specifically sent them to the land of Samaria (Acts 1:8).

G. Followers of John the Baptist. John the Baptist was born of an elderly couple descended from the priestly family of Aaron. Some scholars believe that John went into the desert to live with the Essenes when his parents died (cf. Luke 1:80). More likely, his parents took him to the desert to escape Herod's slaughter of the Jewish baby boys (Matt. 2:16). At any rate, the Essenes may have influenced John's family.

John proclaimed that the Messiah was about to appear in Israel, and he challenged his people to prepare for the coming Redeemer. This drew the attention of the common people, who came to John to be baptized. But Herod feared that John was trying to inspire rebellion (Josephus, *Antiquities,* Bk. XVIII, Chap. V, Sect. 2).

John's teaching indeed seemed revolutionary. He admonished his followers to share their food and clothing (Luke 3:11). He condemned Herod's marriage to his sister-in-law while his brother was still alive. He was not afraid to challenge the political *status quo*. Finally he was executed under the orders of Herod Antipas.

Many of John's followers believed he was the Messiah himself. Even though they did not form a sect in the strictest sense of the word, they constituted an important religious movement in Jesus' day. In the modern Near East, a small sect known as the Mandeans claims to have descended from these followers of John the Baptist.

JESUS' RESPONSE TO THE SECTS

By the first century, the sects of Israel had changed the character of the Jewish faith. The straight and narrow course that God had set before Israel had become a winding path through Oriental mysticism, Greek humanism, and ritualistic traditions. Jesus sought to "make straight" the confusion of the Jewish sects. He spent much of His time responding to the misguided ideas of these groups. Jesus confronted these traditional sources of authority with a truer understanding of the Law. He introduced Israel to the salvation and love of God, alongside His authority. He met the claims to righteousness, which each group made, by declaring all of the sects to be sinners.

Jesus said that a person's righteousness should exceed that of the Pharisees (Matt. 5:20). He warned his disciples to "beware . . . of the leaven [the doctrine] of the Pharisees and of the Sadducees" (Matt. 16:6). He denounced the scribes and Pharisees for their hypocrisy and self-righteousness (Matt. 23:1-36). He especially chided the Pharisees for their superficial methods of observing the Sabbath (Mark 2:23–3:6).

Over and over again, Jesus challenged the religious authorities of His day. He said He came not to abolish the Law, but to fulfill it—suggesting that the Pharisees and Sadducees had already attempted to abolish the Law by their interpretations.

The New Testament never shows Jesus speaking directly to Essenes. But it is likely that their own system of authority had displaced the authority of God and the coming Messiah, as the other Jewish sects had done. They needed to hear Jesus' message of truth, no less than the other Jews did.

6
JESUS CHRIST

The New Testament is the only substantial first-century source of information about the life of Jesus. He is hardly mentioned in Jewish or Roman literature of that time.

The first-century Jewish historian Flavius Josephus wrote a book on the history of Judaism, attempting to show the Romans that Judaism was really not so far distant from the Greek and Roman way of life. Josephus said:

"Now there was about this time Jesus, a wise man, if it be lawful to call him a man, for he was a doer of wonderful works, a teacher of such men as receive the truth with pleasure. He drew over to him both many of the Jews and many of the Gentiles, He was [the] Christ. And when Pilate, at the suggestion of the principal men among us, had condemned him to the cross, those that loved him at the first did not forsake him; for he appeared to them alive again the third day; as the divine things concerning him. And the tribe of Christians so named from him are not extinct to this day."[1]

The Roman biographer Suetonius wrote during Nero's reign:

"Punishment [by Nero] was inflicted on the Christians, a class of men given to a new and mischievous superstition."[2]

A distinguished historian of the second century, Tacitus, remarked that Nero attempted to blame the burning of Rome on the Christians. "But the pernicious superstition, repressed for a time, broke out again," he wrote, "not only through Judea, where the mischief originated, but through the city of Rome also. . . ."[3]

The Roman writer Lucian scorned Christians and described Christ as "the man who was crucified in Palestine because he introduced this new cult into the world."[4]

Bethlehem. This small city 10 km. (6 mi.) south of Jerusalem was the birthplace of David and Jesus. The Old Testament prophet Micah had predicted that the Messiah would be born in this city (Micah 5:2).

Bear in mind that these remarks about Christ and Christianity came from men who were hostile to Christianity and not well-informed about it. Yet they show us that Christianity was widespread by the early second century A.D., and that the historical existence of Christ was accepted as a fact, even by His enemies. Apparently they viewed Him as a religious fanatic who had gained more of a following than He really deserved.

The 4 Gospels are our only primary sources of information about Jesus Christ. They do not present a biography covering His life, but a picture of His person and work. From His birth to His thirtieth year hardly anything is said of Him. Even the account of His ministry is not exhaustive. Much of what John knew and saw, for example, is left unrecorded (John 21:25). What is recorded is sometimes compressed into a few verses. All of the Gospels give considerably more coverage to the events of the last week of Christ's life than they do to anything else.

Because each writer wished to emphasize a somewhat different aspect of Christ's person and work, the accounts vary in detail. It is evident that the original authors selected the facts that best furthered their purposes, and they did not always observe a strictly chronological order. (It is usually assumed that Luke comes nearest to following the actual sequence of events.) The Gospels are more interpretations than chronicles, but there is no reason to doubt that everything they state is completely true.

THE ACCOUNT OF JESUS' LIFE

Though each Gospel was written to stand on its own merits, the 4 Gospels may be worked together into a *harmony*, or single account, of Christ's life. Jesus lived in a Jewish society guided by the Old Testament and basically under the influences of the Pharisaic interpretation of the Law. *(See* chapter 5, "Jews in New Testament Times.")

The Jews of Jesus' day lived in expectation of great events. They were oppressed by the Romans, but strongly convinced that the Messiah would soon come. Various groups pictured the Messiah differently, but hardly a Jew of that day lived without hope in some form. Some in the nation had true faith and looked for the coming of a Messiah who would be their spiritual Savior—e.g., Zechariah and Elisabeth, Simeon, Anna, Joseph and Mary (Luke 1:2; Matt. 1:18ff.). To such faithful hearts came the first stirrings of the Spirit, preparing them for the birth of God's true Messiah, Jesus Christ (Luke 2:27, 36).

About the year 6 B.C., toward the end of Herod's reign in Israel, the priest Zechariah was officiating in the temple of Jerusalem. He was burning incense at the altar during the evening prayer when an angel appeared to him, announcing the forthcoming birth of his first child, a son. This child would prepare the way for the Messiah; the spirit and power of Elijah would rest upon him (cf. Luke 3:3-6). His parents were to call him John. Zechariah was a truly godly man but it was difficult for him to believe what he heard and consequently he was struck dumb until Elisabeth (his wife) gave birth. The child was born, circumcised, and named according to the directions of God. Then Zechariah regained his voice and praised the Lord; this hymn of praise is called the *Benedictus* (Luke 1:5-25, 27-80).

Three months before the birth of John, the same angel (Gabriel) appeared to Mary. This young woman was betrothed to Joseph, a carpenter descended from King David (cf. Isa. 11:1). The angel told Mary she would conceive a child by the Holy Spirit, and that she would name the child Jesus. Mary learned to her amazement that although she was a virgin she would have a child who was the very Son of God and the Savior of His people (Luke 1:32-35; cf. Matt. 1:21). Yet she accepted this message with great meekness, glad to be living in God's will (Luke 1:38).

Gabriel also told her that her cousin Elisabeth was pregnant, and Mary hastened to share their mutual joy. When these two godly women met, Elisabeth greeted Mary as the mother of her Lord (Luke 1:39-45). Mary also broke forth in a song of praise (the *Magnificat,* Luke 1:46-56). She stayed three months with Elisabeth before returning home.

Joseph, Mary's betrothed husband, was utterly shocked at what appeared to be the fruit of terrible sin on Mary's part (Matt. 1:19). He decided to put her away quietly. Then an angel in a dream explained the situation to him, and directed him to marry his intended wife as planned.

Jesus was born in Bethlehem to which the newlyweds had been summoned by the command of the emperor, Augustus Caesar (Luke 2:1). Thus the prophecy of Micah 5:2 was fulfilled.

From everywhere in the empire, Jews had to return to their ancestral cities to be registered so that they might be taxed. This census was taken while Cyrenius (Quirinius) was governor of Syria for the first time. Upon their arrival in Bethlehem, Mary and Joseph were unable to find any housing except a stable (perhaps a cave used to house cattle). There the eternal Son of God was born. He was wrapped in baby clothes and laid in a manger. Soon after His birth, shepherds came to see the child; angels had announced His birth to them while they were tending their flocks. Otherwise mankind had not noticed this event.

A. Early Years. We know of 5 events in the childhood of Jesus. First, in accordance with Jewish Law, He was circumcised and named on the eighth day (Luke 2:21). It is significant that the sinless son of God would undergo this rite binding Him to obedience under the divine covenant and identifying Him with God's people, Israel.

Second, Jesus was presented at the temple to seal the circumcision. He was also "redeemed" by the payment of the presented 5 shekels. For her purification, Mary gave the offering of the poor (cf. Lev. 12:8; Luke 2:24). The mission of Jesus was attested at this time by two godly individuals, Simeon and Anna (Luke 2:25-38).

Third, sometime later a group of "wise men" (perhaps Babylonian priests and astrologers) appeared in Jerusalem, inquiring about the birth of a "King of the Jews." They had seen His star in the sky (Matt. 2:2). Ruthless Herod was immediately alarmed. Having learned from the scribes where prophecy said the Messiah was to be born, he sent the wise men to Bethlehem, asking them to return if they found the Messiah there. Herod claimed that he, too, wanted to worship Him. Actually, he wanted to locate the Christ child so he could remove yet another rival. However, an angel told the wise men not to go back to Herod. Before they arrived in Bethlehem the star reappeared and stood over the place where Jesus and His parents now lived (Matt. 2:9).

Fourth, after the departure of the wise men, God directed Joseph to flee to Egypt with his family. Herod had ordered the execution of all infants aged two and younger who lived in and around Bethlehem. Soon Herod died and God instructed Joseph to return to Nazareth.

The fifth event was Jesus' trip with his parents to the temple when He was 12 years old (Luke 2:41-52). There at the Passover He probably was inducted into the court of the men by being presented to the religious leaders. Unlike His peers, Jesus returned to the temple and continued discussion with the religious teachers (rabbis). He was so engrossed that He did not know His family had departed for home. Amid the confusion of the large group of people with whom they had traveled, His parents were not immediately aware of His absence. When they discovered He was not with them, they returned to Jerusalem and found Him in the temple. When they asked Jesus why He had remained behind, He told them that this was His Father's house and He was about His Father's business.

Scripture says that as a youth Jesus "increased in wisdom and stature, and in favor with God and man" (Luke 2:52).

John the Baptist, Elisabeth's son and Jesus' cousin, was to prepare the way for the ministry of Jesus. He was known as the "Baptist" because he preached to his fellow Jews that they should repent and be baptized. John was a Nazarite (one who was pledged to deny himself the luxuries of society and human comforts to demonstrate his love for God). When Jesus was about 30, He went to John to be baptized. However, He repented of no sin, for He had none. He identified with sinners in order to be their sin-bearer. When Jesus came up from the water, the Holy Spirit visibly descended upon Him in the form of a dove. At least Jesus and John (and perhaps the onlookers as well) heard the voice of God stating His approval of Jesus (Matt. 3:13-17; Mark 1:9-11; Luke 3:21-22; John 1:32-33).

The Holy Spirit at once led Jesus into the wilderness to face

**Traditional site of the tempta-
tion.** An old Greek Orthodox monastery clings to the cliff on Jebel Qarantal, the traditional Mountain of the Temptation west of Jericho. *Qarantal* is an Arabic corruption of the Latin word *quarantana*—"forty days"—in memory of Christ's forty-day fast during His temptation (Matt. 4:1-11).

The Date of Christmas

Nearly 2000 years ago, shepherds in a field near Bethlehem were startled awake by a spectacle never before seen or heard. Wintry clouds were thrust asunder as a heavenly choir burst into majestic song. An angel proclaimed, "We are here to announce the first annual Christmas, which hereafter shall be celebrated throughout the world on December 25."

Fact? Certainly not!

Luke records that angels did announce the birth of "a Savior which is Christ the Lord." And it is true that shepherds received this news. But was the declaration made for December 25?

The fact is that Christmas, as we know it, is a rather modern innovation. Christ's birthday was not celebrated until more than 300 years had gone by, years in which accurate birth records (if there were any) had been lost. The early church remembered and celebrated Christ's Resurrection from the dead, which was more important. But the church was slow in adding Christmas to its list of dates worthy of recognition.

Luke pinpoints the era of Christ's birth by naming Augustus as Rome's imperial ruler. Roman history shows that Caesar Augustus was born 691 years after founding of the city of Rome. Luke 2 further tells that Cyrenius was Syria's governor; again, thanks to Rome's exhaustive record of names and events, historians have determined what is believed to be the particular census that Luke described. These dates have minor discrepancies; yet secular history gives us almost the exact year of Christ's birth.

But the month? the day? Winter was wet and chilly in Judea. It is unlikely that shepherds would have spent a December night in an open field, subject to rain and wind. Christ's birth was more likely during the spring lambing season, when nights would have been balmy and shepherds would have needed to be awake, tending the ewes.

So why have we celebrated Christ's birthday on December 25? A pagan festival, *Natalis Invicti,* was a boisterous Roman affair celebrated on December 25, when the sun was in its winter solstice. Worshipers of the Roman sun god enthusiastically pulled their Christian friends into the partying. By A.D. 386, church leaders set up the celebration of "Christ Mass" ("Christ's Coming"), so that Christians could join the festival activities without bending to paganism.

After the Roman Empire dissolved, Christians continued the December 25 birthday custom. By that time, December 25 seemed more fitting than any other date.

---

temptation by the Devil (Matt. 4:1-11; Mark 1:12-13; Luke 4:1-13). Jesus was alone with His Father and the Holy Spirit while He fasted. But the Devil was also there, tempting Him to (1) satisfy His own hunger, thereby demonstrating distrust of the Father, (2) seize dominion of the world before the Father gave it to Him, and (3) test God to see if He would save Jesus from self-indulged danger, thereby indulging His own self-will.

B. Early Judean Ministry. Only the Gospel of John describes this period of Jesus' life. John first recounts the relationship between Christ and John the Baptist. John the Baptist told delegates from the highest religious authorities that he was not the Messiah, though indicating that the Messiah was present (John 1:19-27). The next day, seeing Jesus approaching he pointed Him out as the Messiah (John 1:30-34). He said, "Behold the Lamb of God . . . ," implying that his own disciples should follow Jesus (John 1:35-37).

Jesus began to gather disciples to Himself (John 1:38-51). As a result of John the Baptist's testimony, John and Andrew turned to Him. Peter became a follower as a result of his brother's testimony. The fourth follower, Philip, immediately obeyed Jesus' summons to him. Philip brought Nathanael (Bartholomew) to Christ, and when Christ demonstrated that He knew Nathanael's inner thoughts, he also joined the band.

Jesus soon journeyed to Galilee. At a wedding feast in Cana, He turned water into wine (the first recorded miracle). This act revealed to the disciples His authority over nature. After a brief ministry in Capernaum, Jesus and His followers went to Jerusalem for the Passover. There He publicly declared His authority over the worship of men by cleansing the temple.[5] At this time Jesus first hinted at His own death and resurrection: "Destroy this temple and in three days I will raise it up again" (John 2:19).

One of the Jewish leaders, a Pharisee named Nicodemus, came to Jesus by night to talk with Him about spiritual matters. Their well-known conversation focused on the necessity of being "born again" (John 3).

The next 6 months found Jesus ministering outside Jerusalem, but still in Judea where John the Baptist was also working. Gradually people began to leave John and follow Jesus. This bothered the Baptist's disciples, but not John himself; he no doubt rejoiced to see the Messiah gaining attention (John 3:27-30).

Toward the end of this 6 months the Baptist was thrown into prison because he denounced Herod Antipas for taking the wife of his brother Philip (Matt. 14:3-5).

Perhaps John's imprisonment prompted Jesus to go to Galilee to minister. At any rate, He went there. On the way He talked with a Samaritan woman He met at a well. Apparently this woman and some of her countrymen accepted Him as the true Messiah and Savior—a most remarkable thing (John 4:1-42). (For the hatred between Samaritans and Jews, *see* chapter 5, "Jews in New Testament Times.")

C. Galilean Ministry. Jesus' first stop on His return to Galilee was at Cana. There He healed a nobleman's son. The fervency of the nobleman persuaded Jesus to fulfill his request (John 4:45-54). In Nazareth Jesus worshiped in the synagogue on the Sabbath. There He was asked to read (in Hebrew) and explain (perhaps in Aramaic) a portion of Scripture. At first His kinsmen were pleased, but they became angry when they realized He was proclaiming Himself the Messiah. They led Him out of the city to cast Him off a precipice, but Jesus passed "through the midst of them" (Luke 4:30) and escaped.

Then Jesus went to Capernaum, which seems to have become His headquarters (cf. Matt. 9:1). Here He officially called to travel with Him the disciples Peter, Andrew, James, and John, who seem to have returned to their homes and occupations. Jesus taught in the synagogue each Sabbath and healed a demoniac there. He also healed Peter's mother-in-law (Matt. 8:14-15; Mark 1:29-31; Luke 4:38; cf. 1 Cor. 9:5). A crowd of sick folk subsequently gathered, "and he laid his hands on every one of them, and healed them" (Luke 4:40).

In the next stage of Jesus' ministry, He found great popularity among the common people. Now Jesus' primary mission was teaching, so He turned His back on those who would keep him chained to one spot for a ministry of healing only (Luke 4:42-44; cf. Mark 1:35, 37). The people acclaimed His miracles and teaching. Typical of His work on this circuit was the healing of the leper (Luke 5:12-15; cf. Mark 1:40-45). This incident underscored Jesus' submission to the Law, His compassion for men, and His interest in bringing men to salvation. (He commanded the leper to make the long journey to Jerusalem and present himself in the temple for the prescribed purification, submitting himself to God.)

Back in Capernaum, Jesus demonstrated His authority to forgive sin by curing a paralytic and summoning Matthew, a much-hated tax collector, to become His follower (Luke

5:16-29). Matthew responded immediately. During a feast at Matthew's house, scribes and Pharisees criticized Jesus and His disciples for their self-indulgence. Jesus responded that they were rejoicing at the presence of the Messiah, not revelling in self-indulgence. He alluded to His death and the mourning that would accompany it. But He promised that the mourning would be short-lived, for the spirit of the gospel could not be confined to the "old wineskins" of Jewish legalism (Luke 4:30-39).

During this period Jesus began to meet increasing hostility from the high Jewish officials. While in Jerusalem for one of the Jews' annual feasts, He was attacked for healing a cripple on the Sabbath (John 5:1-16). He thus asserted His authority

Pilate Inscription. Discovered in 1961 in the ruins of the Roman theater at Caesarea, this inscription mentions the names of the Emperor Tiberius and Pontius Pilate, who served as governor of Judea from A.D. 26 to 36. The most recent reading of the inscription is: "In honor of Julius Tiberius/Marcus Pontius Pilate/prefect of Judea."

over the Sabbath and the Jews at once understood this to be a claim for divine authority. Jesus said that He knew God's mind, that He would judge sin, and that He would raise people from the dead. His critics pointed out that only God can do such things.

Back in Galilee, the Sabbath controversy continued as Jesus defended His disciples for picking grain on the Sabbath. Ultimately He claimed divine Lordship over the day. He healed a man with a withered hand on the Sabbath. The Jewish religious authorities began plotting to destroy Him (Matt. 12:1-14; Mark 2:23-3:6; Luke 6:1-11).

Now Jesus singled out 12 of His disciples who were officially to carry on His ministry. The appointment of the Twelve inaugurated a new period of Christ's ministry, beginning with our version of the great Sermon on the Mount. Jesus delivered this message (also called the Sermon on the Plain) when He descended from the mountain with His newly appointed apostles (Luke 6:20-49; cf. Matt. 5:1-6:29).

Now we read of several interwoven incidents. Perhaps on the very day He delivered the Sermon on the Mount, Jesus healed a centurion's servant. This centurion, a Roman soldier, was sympathetic toward the Jewish religion (Luke 7:5) and apparently embraced Jesus as the true Messiah. The servant was healed "in the selfsame hour" that the centurion made his request (Matt. 8:5-13; cf. Luke 7:1-10).

At Capernaum, perhaps about 11 km. (7 mi.) from the site of the Sermon on the Mount, crowds continued to press upon Jesus. To escape this pressure, He set out for Nain (with many accompanying Him). At the city's entrance He restored a widow's son to life. This incident stirred the excitement of the crowd (Luke 7:11-15).

About this time messengers from John the Baptist came to ask Jesus if He was really the Messiah. Still imprisoned, John had grown perplexed with the course of Jesus' ministry; it was peaceful and merciful, rather than dramatic, conquering, and judgmental. Jesus commended John and denounced the Jewish authorities who had opposed him—indeed, He pointed out that the cities of Galilee that heard John had "repented not." They had not truly "come unto Him" (Matt. 11:20-24; Luke 7:18-35; cf. 10:12-21).

In one of the cities Jesus visited (perhaps Nain), He was anointed by an outcast woman. He forgave her sins in the presence of His host, Simon the Pharisee. Simon was scandalized, but Jesus was happy to receive her love (Matt. 26:6-13; Mark 14:3-9; Luke 7:36-50).

This brings us to Jesus' second tour of the Galilean cities (Luke 8:1-4). The Twelve and certain devoted women (Mary Magdalene; Joanna, wife of Herod's steward; Susanna; and "many others") accompanied Him. It was on this journey that He cured the demoniac and the Pharisees accused Him of being in league with the devil. For this, Jesus strongly rebuked them (Matt. 8:28-34; Mark 5:1-20; Luke 8:26-39). He emphasized the blessedness of those who "hear the word of God and do it" (Luke 8:21). This same day He spoke many parables from a boat. The parable became Jesus' primary teaching tool, which both revealed and hid the truths He wanted to communicate (Mark 4:10-12; Luke 8:9-10). No doubt He repeated this and other sayings in different contexts, much as present-day ministers repeat their sermons and illustrations.

After preaching from the boat, Jesus crossed over the Sea of Galilee to the western shore. Before He departed, two men approached Him and asked to become His disciples (Matt. 8:18-22). But each made his request in an unrealistic and unworthy way, and Jesus rebuked them.

While crossing the sea, Jesus' life was threatened by a violent storm. He was asleep on a cushion in the stern of the boat, and so His disciples awakened Him. At once He stilled the storm, and the disciples exclaimed, "What manner of man is this! for he commandeth even the winds and water, and they obey Him" (Luke 8:25; cf. Mark 4:35-44).

On the other side of Galilee, Jesus met a demoniac and drove the demons from him into a herd of swine, which immediately plunged to their death in the sea. When the townspeople came out to meet Christ, they found the demoniac fully clothed and in his right mind. Surprisingly, they begged Jesus to leave. He did so after He had sent the man to tell his friends of the Messiah (Matt. 8:28; Mark 5:1-20).

We are told of two miracles that Jesus performed when He returned to Capernaum: He raised Jairus' daughter from the dead and cured a woman with an issue of blood when she touched the hem of His garment (Matt. 9:18-26; Mark 5:21-43; Luke 8:40-56).

Jesus made a third tour of Galilee that included a number of miracles and a second rejection at Nazareth. Jesus yearned for more laborers to reap the spiritual harvest. He sent His disciples two-by-two to call the cities of Israel to repentance, granting them power to heal and cast out demons. Thus their ministry extended His own (Matt. 10:5-15; Mark 6:7-13; Luke 9:1-6).

At this point, we read the report of John the Baptist's death. Herod Antipas had long hesitated before killing John because he feared the people; but his wife Herodias plotted John's death using her daughter Salome to achieve her goal. Herod's guilty conscience led him to ask if Jesus was the resurrected John.

Grieving at John's death, beleaguered by crowds, and exhausted from work, Jesus gathered the Twelve and crossed the Sea of Galilee. But the crowds got there before them, and Jesus taught the masses all day. The session was climaxed when Jesus fed the entire multitude (5,000 men) by dividing and multiplying five loaves and two fish. When the leftovers were gathered they filled twelve baskets (Matt. 14:13-21).

Immediately after the miracle Jesus put the Twelve into the boat and sent them back across the Sea of Galilee, even though a storm was brewing. He retreated into the mountains to escape the overly enthusiastic crowd, which wanted to make Him king by force. Three hours after midnight, the disciples were caught in a violent storm in the middle of the lake. They were frightened. But when disaster seemed certain, Jesus came walking toward them on the water (Matt. 14:22-36; Mark 6:45-56). After He calmed their fears, Peter asked Jesus if He would permit him to come and meet Him. On the way, Peter lost heart and began to sink. Jesus took his hand and led him back to the boat. The water was calmed immediately.

In Capernaum Jesus began to heal the sick who streamed to Him from everywhere. Soon the crowd who had been fed arrived. Finding Jesus in a synagogue, they heard Him explain that He was the true bread of life from heaven.

They were now faced with accepting the authority of this teaching, spelled out in terms of eating Jesus' flesh and drinking His blood. This offended many of them and they left (John 6:22-66). Jesus asked the Twelve if they too were going to leave. This elicited Peter's well-known confession, "Lord, to whom shall we go? . . . We believe and are sure that thou art that Christ, the Son of the living God" (John 6:69).

After His discourse on the bread of life, Jesus turned from public teaching and devoted Himself to instructing His disciples (Matt. 15:1-20; Mark 7:1-23). The Jewish authorities resented Jesus' rejection of their religious ceremonies and His bold rebuke of their claims to authority. Jesus moved from place to place, seeking to avoid public exposure; but He could not always do this. In the area of Tyre and Sidon He healed a Gentile's daughter (Matt. 15:21-28), and in Decapolis He healed many who were brought to Him by the crowds (Matt. 15:29-31). He fed 4,000 people by multiplying loaves and a few fish (Matt. 15:32-39; Mark 8:1-10).

Back in the area of Capernaum. He was again besieged by the Jewish religious officials. To escape, He took a boat across the Sea of Galilee again. On the way He warned the Twelve of the Pharisees, Sadducees, and Herod (Matt. 16:1-12; Mark 8:11-21). In Bethsaida Jesus healed a blind man (Mark 8:22-26). Then He and His disciples journeyed north to the area of Caesarea Philippi, where Peter confessed Him to be the Messiah, "the Christ, the Son of the living God." Jesus replied that Peter's faith made him a rock, and that He would build His church upon this rock—that is, faith such as Peter had (Matt. 16:13-20; cf. Mark 8:27–9:1). At this point Jesus described His approaching suffering, death, and resurrection.

About a week later, Jesus took Peter, James, and John up a mountain and revealed to them His heavenly glory (the Transfiguration). He conversed before their eyes with Moses and Elijah (Matt. 17:1-13; Mark 9:2-13; cf. Luke 9:28-36). At the foot of the mountain Jesus healed a demon-possessed boy whom the disciples had been unable to help (Matt. 17:14-23; Mark 9:14-32; Luke 9:37-44).

Jesus again toured Galilee but this time secretly. He again told the Twelve of His coming death and resurrection, and again they were unable to receive what He said.

Jesus paid the temple tax with money that was miraculously provided. On the way to Capernaum, He taught the disciples concerning the true nature of greatness and forgiveness (Matt. 17:22–18:35).

After many months, Jesus went to Jerusalem to celebrate the Feast of Tabernacles. He had refused to go with His family but later He made the trip privately. In Jerusalem the people's opinions about Him were divided. Jesus publicly affirmed that He was sent from the Father; He was the Messiah, the Savior of the world. The top religious authorities sent officers to arrest Jesus, but they were so impressed by Him that they were unable to fulfill their task. Then the religious authorities attempted to discredit Him by getting Him to violate the Law. But they were not successful. They brought to Him a woman taken in adultery and He completely turned the incident against them (John 8:1-11).

During this period Nicodemus tried to calm the hatred of the Sanhedrin (the high council of Jewish religious authorities). But while Jesus was in Jerusalem, He healed a blind man on the Sabbath. This provoked a great controversy and the man was cast out of the synagogue (a terrible disgrace). Jesus found the man, who recognized Him as the Messiah

Ankle bone and spike. An iron spike driven through the ankle bone of a thirty-year-old man is the result of a first-century crucifixion, a practice that the Greeks and Romans adopted from the Phoenicians. Roman citizens were exempt from the cruel punishment, which was reserved for slaves and rebels. Death came very painfully and very slowly, occasionally taking as long as 9 days.

(John 9). Here Jesus delivered His famous discourse on the Good Shepherd (John 10:1-21).

D. Perean Ministry. About two months elapsed while Jesus went back to Galilee. Perhaps it was at this time that He sent 70 disciples into the cities of Israel to declare that the Kingdom was near and that Jesus was the Messiah (Luke 10). Jesus attempted to pass through Samaria on His way to Jerusalem, but the people rejected Him. So He crossed the Jordan and traveled through Perea. At one point a lawyer asked Jesus what he needed to do to inherit eternal life. Jesus told him to love God and his neighbor, to which the lawyer replied, "Who is my neighbor?" (Luke 10:28). Then Jesus told him the famous parable of the Good Samaritan. During this journey Jesus performed many miracles, such as healing an infirm woman and a dropsied man on the Sabbath (Luke 13:11-17; 14:1-6). The Sabbath miracles stirred yet more hostility among the Pharisees.

Then the scene shifted to Judea. Perhaps this was the time Jesus visited Bethany and the home of Mary and Martha. Mary sat at Jesus' feet while Martha prepared the meal. Martha complained about her sister's idleness, but Jesus answered that Mary had chosen "that good part"—i.e., listening to His teaching while He was still on earth (Luke 10:42). In Jerusalem at the annual Feast of Dedication, Jesus openly declared Himself to be the Messiah. The Jews regarded this as blasphemy, and they again tried to seize Him. Jesus then retreated across the Jordan to Bethabara. But the opposition of the religious authorities continued to grow.

The outcasts of society rallied to hear His teaching. Again He taught primarily in parables. Jesus privately explained the true meaning of His parables to the Twelve and otherwise continued their special training. One day an urgent message arrived from the home of Mary and Martha: Lazarus, their brother, was mortally ill. By the time Jesus arrived in Bethany, Lazarus had been dead and buried for 4 days. But Jesus raised Him from the tomb. This miracle increased the determination of the religious authorities to get rid of Him (John 11:1-46).

Jesus again retired from the crowds for a time. Then He turned His face toward Jerusalem and death (John 11:54-57). The way to Jerusalem was marked by miracle working, teaching, and confrontation with the Pharisees. While He was on this journey, several parents brought their infants to Jesus for His blessing (Luke 18:15-17). He urged a "rich young ruler" to forsake his wealth and follow Him (Luke 18:18-30). And He again told His disciples of His coming death (Luke 18:31-34). In anticipation of that event, He described the rewards of the Kingdom and instructed His disciples to be servants of their people (Matt. 20:1-16). In the vicinity of Jericho, Jesus healed some blind men, among whom was Bartimaeus, who recognized Jesus as the Messiah (Mark 10:46-52). He ate in the home of Zaccheus the publican, who also received salvation through faith in Him (Luke 19:1-10). From Jericho Jesus went to the home of Lazarus, Mary, and Martha in Bethany.

E. The Last Week. The last week before Jesus' crucifixion occupies a large portion of the Gospel records. Jesus attended a feast in Jericho at the home of Simon the leper, where Mary anointed Him with costly perfumes and wiped His feet with her hair. Judas protested this act because he felt it was a waste of money. But Jesus commended the woman. He pointed out that she was anointing Him for His coming burial (Matt. 26:13; Mark 14:3-9).

On the next day (Sunday), Jesus rode into Jerusalem on a colt upon which His followers had spread their garments (John 12). The Passover pilgrims lined the road, waving palm branches and acclaiming Jesus as the Messiah. When the Pharisees told Jesus to rebuke His followers, He replied that if His followers were quiet the stones would cry out. That evening Jesus and the Twelve returned to Bethany (Matt. 21:1-9; Mark 11:1-10; Luke 19:28-38).

The next day they journeyed once again to Jerusalem. On the way He cursed a fig tree for not having fruit when He required it (Matt. 21:18-19; Mark 11:12-14). By the following morning the fig tree had withered.

On Tuesday the Jewish leaders demanded that Jesus explain the authority by which He acted as He did. Jesus replied by telling several parables. He successfully thwarted the Pharisees' traps to get Him to contradict Moses and be discredited before the crowds. At one point Jesus pointedly denounced the scribes and Pharisees (Matt. 23:1-36). This was followed by an expression of His concern and longing for the people to love Him (Matt. 23:37-39). He also commented on the great sacrifice of the widow's mite (Mark 12:41-44) and talked to some Greeks who had requested an interview (John 12:20). He delivered a discourse on last things (Matt. 24:4–25:15; Mark 13:5-37). Perhaps on Tuesday evening Judas appeared before the council of the Sanhedrin and contracted to betray Jesus for 30 pieces of silver. This bounty was worth less than $20 in today's currency—it was the price of a slave in Jesus' time.

Jesus spent Wednesday resting in Bethany. On Thursday evening He ate the Passover with His disciples (Matt. 26:17-30; Mark 14:12-25). He sent Peter and John to find the place where the meal would be eaten. The feast involved sacrificing a lamb at the temple and eating it while sitting around a table with one's family. Jesus told two of the disciples to meet and follow a man bearing a pitcher who would lead them to the house where the feast would be prepared. They followed Jesus' directions, and the man led them to a house whose owner had already prepared a room for the purpose.

During the meal that evening, the disciples began to argue about which one of them would be most important. Jesus arose and washed their feet, trying to teach them that they should serve one another (John 13:1-17). After the meal Jesus instituted the Lord's Supper, a rite to be observed until He would come again. This symbolic meal consisted of eating bread (representing His body) and drinking wine (representing His blood).

Judas left the meal to finalize his arrangements to betray Jesus. Jesus warned the remaining disciples that they would lose their faith in Him that night. But Peter assured Jesus of his loyalty. Jesus replied that he would deny Him three times before the cock crowed at dawn.

Jesus and His remaining disciples left the Upper Room and went to the Garden of Gethsemane. While Jesus agonized in prayer, the disciples fell asleep. Three times He returned to find them sleeping. Finally He calmed His soul and was ready to face His death and all it would mean (Matt. 26:36-46; Mark 14:32-42). At this point Judas arrived with a company of armed men. He identified Jesus for the soldiers by kissing Him (Matt. 26:47-56; Mark 14:43-52; Luke 22:47-53; John 18:1-14).

Jesus stood trial before both the religious and civil authorities. The religious trial was illegally convened during the night; but it confirmed its decision after daybreak. Even at that, the whole matter was a mockery of justice (Matt. 26:59-68; Mark 14:55-65; Luke 22:65-71).

The civil trial occurred Friday morning before Pilate, who saw no threat or crime in Jesus. He sent Christ to Herod, who mocked Him and returned Him to Pilate (Luke 23:6-16). The Roman official hoped to release Jesus by popular demand but the crowd shouted for him to release Barabbas (a robber and murderer). They insisted that Pilate crucify Christ. Pilate proposed to scourge Christ and release Him to pacify the crowd and he inflicted on Him other mockeries and punishments. But again the crowd cried, "Crucify Him." Ultimately

Thirty Pieces of Silver

One of the most infamous stories of the Bible is that of Judas Iscariot, the disciple who betrayed Christ for thirty pieces of silver. While it is difficult to determine exactly what thirty pieces of silver was worth, we know it was not a fortune.

The Roman *denarius*, was the most common coin used during Jesus' day. Struck from silver, this coin bore an imprint with the head of the emperor. Because of this, the Jewish people were not allowed to use coins as offerings in religious services; they converted their coins to pieces of silver. Money changers converted the *denarius* or *shekel* to silver for a fee of twelve percent.

The denarius would be worth about twenty cents in today's market, according to its silver weight and content. But one denarius equaled a day's wages of a common laborer at that time, so it had significant buying power. Even so, by this estimate we find that Judas betrayed Christ for a month's salary—hardly a fortune.

The Book of Zechariah prophesied that such an amount would be paid for the Messiah (Zech. 11:12). When Judas accepted thirty pieces of silver for the life of Christ, he fulfilled the prophecy (Matt. 26:15). The amount was also the typical price of a slave or servant during that time.

Pilate gave in and sent Jesus to His death. In the midst of all this tumult, Jesus remained calm and composed (Matt. 27:11-31; Mark 15:2-20; Luke 23:2-25; John 18:28–19:15).

From Pilate's court, Jesus was taken outside the walls of Jerusalem to the hill of Golgotha, where He was crucified at about 9 A.M. on Friday. Accounts of Jesus' execution are found in Matthew 27:32-56 and parallel narratives.

Nicodemus and Joseph of Arimathea took Jesus' body and buried it in Joseph's tomb. Pilate sealed the tomb and set a guard over it to make certain the body was not stolen by Jesus' disciples.

Jesus was buried before dark on Friday ("the first day," since the Jews reckoned days from dusk to dusk). His body remained in the tomb from dusk Friday to dusk Saturday ("the second day") and from dusk Saturday to dawn Sunday ("the third day"). On the morning of the third day the astonished soldiers felt the earth quake and saw an angel roll away the stone sealing the tomb. They fled from the scene. Soon a group of women came to anoint Jesus' body with spices. They

Rock-hewn tomb. Similar to the one in which the body of Jesus was laid, this tomb was excavated out of soft limestone rock. The tomb probably contained a first chamber with a ledge around it as a seat and a second chamber with a niche cut into the wall for the body. When the niche was needed for additional bodies, the bones of the first were placed in a hole in the floor. The Gospels state that the tomb of Christ was new (Matt. 27:60; John 19:41), not merely an old tomb that had been emptied.

found the tomb empty. Running back to the city, they reported the news to Jesus' disciples. Peter and John came to the tomb and found it just as they had said (Matt. 27:57–28:10 and parallels). Jesus had risen from the dead.

Jesus appeared to His followers on 10 recorded occasions after His resurrection. At one of these appearances, Jesus commissioned the 11 remaining apostles to go into all the world and make disciples, baptizing and teaching them. This is known as the Great Commission (Matt. 28:19-20). The last time He appeared to His apostles, Christ ascended into heaven (John 24:49-53; Acts 1:6-11). Jesus promised to return just as He had ascended—visibly and physically. (After the Resurrection Jesus had a real body, although it was not limited by time and space.) He again promised the coming of the Holy Spirit. Although the Holy Spirit has come, the church still awaits the second coming of Christ.

THE DOCTRINE OF CHRIST

Christology deals with the person and work of Christ—i.e., the doctrine of Christ.

A. His Person. Understanding Christ's person is no easy task, but there is general agreement on most aspects of the nature of Christ and His personality.

Five titles of Jesus reflect something significant of His person and/or work. The name *Jesus* (which is identical with *Joshua* and means "God is Savior") emphasizes His role as the Savior of His people (Matt. 1:21). *Christ* is the New Testament equivalent of *Messiah,* a Hebrew word meaning "anointed one" (cf. Acts 4:27; 10:38). This title emphasized that Jesus was divinely appointed to His mission, that he had an official relationship to God the Father—that is, He had a job to do and a role to discharge at the Father's appointing.

Son of Man was the title used almost exclusively by Jesus Himself (cf. Matt. 9:6; 10:23; 11:19). Some feel He used it because it most clearly distinguished His Messiahship from the erroneous ideas of His time.

The name *Son of God* was also applied to Jesus in an official or Messianic sense (cf. Matt. 4:3, 6; 16:16; Luke 22:70; John 1:49). It emphasized that He was a Person of the triune Godhead, supernaturally born as a human being.

Lord was alternately applied to Jesus as a simple title (somewhat like "Mr."), a title of authority or ownership, or (sometimes) an indication of His equality with God (e.g., Mark 12:36-37; Luke 2:11; Matt. 7:22).

Today Christians believe that Jesus is both God and man—i.e., that He has two distinct natures united "inconfusedly, unchangeably, indivisibly, inseparably" in His one person (Chalcedonian Creed, A.D. 451).

This doctrine is not built on human reason, but on biblical revelation. There is much scriptural proof that Jesus is divine. Scripture states that there is only one God and no lesser gods (cf. Exod. 20:3-5; Isa. 42:8; 44:6), yet it clearly affirms that Jesus is God (e.g., John 1:1; Rom. 9:5; Heb. 1:8). The Bible reports that Jesus was worshiped at God's command (Heb. 1:6), while lesser spiritual beings refuse to be worshiped (Rev. 22:8–9) because worship was to be rendered only to God. Only the divine Creator may be worshiped by His creatures. But Jesus Christ, God's Son, is co-creator with His Father (John 1:3; Col. 1:16; Heb. 1:2); therefore both must be worshiped. Again, Scripture declares that Jesus was the Savior of His people (Matt. 1:21), even though Jehovah was the only Savior of His people (Isa. 43:11; Hos. 13:4). It states that the Father Himself has clearly called Jesus God (Heb. 1:8).

Scripture also teaches the true humanity of Jesus. The Christ of the New Testament is no illusion or ghost; He is human in every sense. He called Himself man, as did others (e.g., John 8:40; Acts 2:22). He lived in the flesh (John 1:14; 1 Tim. 3:16; 1 John 4:2). He possessed a human body and mind (Luke 23:39; John 11:33; Heb. 2:14). He experienced human wants and sufferings (Luke 2:40, 52; Heb. 2:10, 18; 5:8). However, the Bible emphasizes that Jesus did not partake of the sin that characterizes all other human beings (cf. Luke 1:35; John 8:46; Heb. 4:15).

B. His Personality. Christ has two distinct natures but is a single person, not two persons under one skin. He is the eternal Logos (divine Word), the second person of the Trinity, yet He assumed human nature in such a way that there was no essential change in the divine nature. We can address Christ in prayer using titles that reflect both His human and divine natures, although His divine nature is the ultimate basis of our worship. The incarnation manifested the *triune* (three-in-One) God by showing us the relationship between Father, Son, and Spirit (cf. Matt. 3:16-17; John 14:15-26; Rom. 1:3-4; Gal. 4:4-5; 1 Pet. 1:1-12). Because Jesus is one Person, and because the unity of His personal life embraces all His character and all His powers, Scripture speaks of Him as being both divine and human. It ascribes divine acts and attributes to Christ the eternal Son of God (Acts 20:28).

C. His Position. As we seek to understand Christ, we should examine His position before the Law. He humbled Himself before it; as a result, God exalted Him over it. This is an interesting irony.

The Son laid aside His divine majesty and assumed human nature. He submitted Himself to all the sufferings of His earthly life, including death itself. He did this to accomplish God's plan to redeem mankind from sin.

When the divine Logos became flesh He did not cease to be what He was before. By the same token, the incarnation as such—that is, the Word's bodily existence—continues as He sits at the right hand of God.

Christ was surrounded by sin. The Devil repeatedly attacked Him. His own people hated Him and refused to believe He was the Savior. His enemies persecuted Him. Finally, at the end of His earthly life, He endured all the wrath of God against sin. No other person has suffered as intensely as Jesus did.

God the Father exalted Christ by raising Him from the dead, taking Him away to heaven, and seating Him at His own right hand. Christ will return from that place of honor to judge the living and the dead.

D. His Prophetic Office. The Old Testament depicts a prophet as a person who receives God's Word (revelation) and passes it on to his people. In order to function as a prophet, a person had to receive a clear word from God. He stood in God's stead before the people; God used his mouth to communicate what He wished to say.

The Old Testament promised a great prophet who would convey God's word finally and decisively to His people (Deut. 18:15). Jesus was that prophet (Acts 3:22-24). He acted prophetically even before He came to earth as a man, for He spoke through the writers of the Old Testament (1 Pet. 1:11). During His earthly ministry He taught His followers the things of God, by both word and deed. Now He continues His

Gordon's Calvary. The word *Calvary* (Luke 23:33) comes from a Latin translation of an Aramaic word—the *Golgotha* of Matthew 27:33, meaning "skull." Scripture simply says that Calvary was located outside Jerusalem, that it was fairly conspicuous, and that a garden containing the tomb lay nearby. Two sites—the Church of the Holy Sepulcher and Gordon's Calvary—are possible locations of the Crucifixion. The church marks the older spot, which is supported by tradition that goes back at least to the fourth century. Gordon's Calvary, pictured here, contains a rock formation resembling a skull. This site accords with other biblical data, but there is no tradition to support its claim.

prophetic work from heaven by operating through the Holy Spirit.

E. His Priestly Office. While the Old Testament prophet represented God before the people, the priest represented the people before God. So Christ represents His people before the Father (Heb. 3:1; 4:14).

The Bible tells us that a priest must be appointed by God. He must act on man's behalf in things that pertain to God. For example, He must make sacrifices and offerings for sins, intercede for the people He represents, and bless them (Heb. 5:1; 7:25; cf. Lev. 9:22).

Jesus presented Himself as a priestly sacrifice. The Old Testament sacrifices were *expiatory* (because they "put away" sin, thus restoring the worshiper to the blessings and privileges God intended for him) and *vicarious* (because another life was offered for sin instead of the life of the worshiper). Christ's once-for-all sacrifice was both expiatory and vicarious, and it gained for His people eternal salvation.

Christ reconciles the sinner to God. God expressed His love for mankind by sending Christ to redeem us from our sins (John 3:16). In every event, God has attempted to bring His creatures back to Him. So when Christ came into the world, there was no change in God Himself, only a change in His relation to sinners. Christ's sacrifice covered the guilt that stood between sinners and God.

Christ also intercedes for His people (Heb. 7:25). He entered the Holy Place of heaven by means of the perfect, all-sufficient sacrifice that He offered to the Father. In so doing, He represented those who put their faith in Him and reinstated them before the Father (Heb. 9:24).

In the presence of God, Christ now answers the constant accusations of the devil against believers (Rom. 8:33-34). Our prayers and services are tainted with sin and imperfection; Christ perfects them in the eyes of the Father, speaking constantly to the Father in our behalf. Finally, Christ prays for believers. He pleads for the needs we do not mention in our prayers—things we ignore, underestimate, or do not see. He does this to protect us from danger and sustain us in faith until we attain victory in the end. He also prays for those who have not yet believed. He constantly does this intercessory work.

F. His Kingly Office. As the second person of the Trinity, co-creator with the Father, Christ is the eternal king over all things. As Savior, He is the king of a spiritual kingdom—that is, He rules in the hearts and lives of His people. By reason of His spiritual kingship, Christ is called the "head" of the church (Eph. 1:22).

Christ rules and governs all things on behalf of His church. He will not allow His purposes to be frustrated in the end. Christ received this universal kingship when God exalted Him to His place of honor in heaven. He will deliver this kingdom to the Father when He accomplishes the final victory over evil (1 Cor. 15:24-28)—i.e., when He destroys this world-order once for all and makes it new. Then the universe as we know it will cease to exist. No human kings or diabolical powers will be able to reign. Only Christ and His Kingdom will be preserved.

7

THE APOSTLES

At the beginning of His ministry, Jesus selected twelve men to travel with Him. These men would have an important responsibility: They would continue to represent Him after He had returned to heaven. Their reputation would continue to influence the church long after they were dead.

So the selection of the Twelve was a great responsibility. "And it came to pass in those days, that he went out into a mountain to pray, and continued all night in prayer to God. And when it was day, he called unto him his disciples: and of them he chose twelve, whom he also named apostles" (Luke 6:12-13).

Most of the apostles came from the area of Capernaum, which was despised by polite Jewish society because it was the center of a part of the Jewish state (only recently added) and was known in fact as "Galilee of the Gentiles." Jesus Himself said, "And thou, Capernaum, which art exalted into heaven, shalt be brought down to hell" (Matt. 11:23). Yet Jesus molded these twelve men into strong leaders and articulate spokesmen of the Christian faith. Their success bears witness to the transforming power of Jesus' lordship.

None of the Gospel writers have left us any physical descriptions of the Twelve. Nevertheless, they give us tiny clues that help us to make "educated guesses" about how the apostles looked and acted. One very important fact that has traditionally been overlooked in countless artistic representations of the apostles is their youth. If we realize that most lived into the third and fourth quarter of the century and John into the second century, then they must have been only teenagers when they first took up Christ's call.

Different biblical accounts list the Twelve in pairs. We are not sure whether this indicates family relationships, team functions, or some other kind of association between them.

ANDREW

The day after John the Baptist saw the Holy Spirit descend upon Jesus, he identified Jesus for two of his disciples and said, "Behold the Lamb of God!" (John 1:36). Intrigued by this announcement, the two men left John and began to follow Jesus. Jesus noticed them and asked what they were seeking. Immediately they replied, "Rabbi, where dwellest thou?" Jesus took them to the house where He was staying and they spent the night with Him. One of these men was named Andrew (John 1:38-40).

Andrew soon went to find his brother, Simon Peter. He told Peter, "We have found the Messiah . . ." (John 1:41). Through his testimony, he won Peter to the Lord.

Andrew is our English rendering of the Greek word *Andreas,* which means "manly." Other clues from the Gospels indicate that Andrew was physically strong and a devout, faithful man. He and Peter owned a house together (Mark 1:29). They were sons of a man named Jonah or John, a prosperous fisherman. Both of the young men had followed their father into the fishing business.

Andrew was born at Bethsaida on the northern shores of the Sea of Galilee. Though the Gospel of John describes Andrew's first encounter with Jesus, it does not mention him as a disciple until much later (John 6:8). The Gospel of Matthew says that when Jesus was walking along the Sea of Galilee He hailed Andrew and Peter and invited them to become His disciples (Matt. 4:18-19). This does not contradict John's narrative; it simply adds a new feature. A close reading of John 1:35-40 shows that Jesus did not call Andrew and Peter to follow Him the first time they met.

Andrew and another disciple named Philip introduced a group of Greek men to Jesus (John 12:20-22). For this reason, we might say that Andrew and Philip were the first foreign missionaries of the Christian faith.

Tradition says that Andrew spent his last years in Scythia, north of the Black Sea. But a small book entitled the *Acts of Andrew* (probably written about A.D. 260) says that he preached primarily in Macedonia and was martyred at Patras.[1]

Roman Catholic tradition says that Andrew was crucified on an X-shaped cross, a religious symbol that is now known as St. Andrew's Cross. It was believed that he was crucified on November 30, so the Roman Catholic church and Greek Orthodox church observe his festival on that date. Today he is the patron saint of Scotland. The Order of St. Andrew is an association of church ushers who make a special effort to be courteous to strangers.

BARTHOLOMEW (NATHANAEL)

We lack information about the identity of the apostle named Bartholomew. He is mentioned only in the lists of apostles. Moreover, while the Synoptic Gospels agree that his name was Bartholomew, John gives it as Nathanael (John 1:45). Some scholars believe that Bartholomew was the surname of Nathanael.

The Aramaic word *bar* means "son," so the name *Bartholomew* literally meant "son of Thalmai." The Bible does not identify Thalmai for us, but he may have been named after the King Thalmai of Geshur (2 Sam. 3:3). Some scholars believe that Bartholomew was connected with the Ptolemies, the ruling family of Egypt; this theory is based upon Jerome's statement that Bartholomew was the only apostle of noble birth.

Assuming that Bartholomew is the same person as Nathanael, we learn a bit more about his personality from the Gospel of John. Jesus called Nathanael "an Israelite . . . in whom is no guile" (John 1:47).

Tradition says Nathanael served as a missionary in India. The Venerable Bede said that Nathanael was beheaded by King Astriagis. Other traditions say that Nathanael was crucified head-down.

JAMES, SON OF ALPHEUS

The Gospels make only fleeting reference to James, the son of Alpheus (Matt. 10:3; Mark 3:18; Luke 6:15). Many scholars believe that James was a brother of Matthew, since Scripture says that Matthew's father was also named Alpheus (Mark 2:14). Others believe that this James was identified with "James the Less"; but we have no proof that these two names refer to the same man (cf. Mark 15:40).

If the son of Alpheus was indeed the same man as James the Less, he may have been a cousin of Jesus (cf. Matt. 27:56; John 19:25). Some Bible commentators theorize that this disciple bore a close physical resemblance to Jesus, which could explain why Judas Iscariot had to identify Jesus on the night of His betrayal (Mark 14:43-45; Luke 22:47-48).

Legends say that this James preached in Persia and was crucified there. But we have no concrete information about his later ministry and death.

JAMES, SON OF ZEBEDEE

After Jesus summoned Simon Peter and his brother Andrew, He went a little farther along the shore of Galilee and summoned "James the son of Zebedee and John his brother, who also were in the ship mending their nets" (Mark 1:19). Like Peter and Andrew, James and his brother responded immediately to Christ's invitation.

James was the first of Twelve to suffer a martyr's death. King Herod Agrippa I ordered that James be executed with a sword (Acts 12:2). Tradition says this occurred in A.D. 44, when James would have been quite young. (Although the New

Testament does not describe the martyrdom of any other apostles, tradition tells us that all except John died for their faith.)

The Gospels never mention James alone; they always speak of "James and John." Even in recording his death, the Book of Acts refers to him as "James the brother of John" (Acts 12:2). James and John began to follow Jesus on the same day, and both of them were present at the transfiguration of Jesus (Mark 9:2-13). Jesus called both men the "sons of thunder" (Mark 3:17).

The persecution that took James' life inspired new fervor among the Christians (cf. Acts 12:5-25). Undoubtedly, Herod Agrippa had hoped to quash the Christian movement by executing leaders such as James. "But the Word of God grew and multiplied" (v. 24).

Strangely, the Gospel of John does not mention James. John was reluctant to mention his own name, and he may have felt the same kind of modesty about reporting the activities of his brother. Once John refers to himself and James as the "sons of Zebedee" (John 21:2). Otherwise he is silent about the work of James.

Legends say that James was the first Christian missionary to Spain. Roman Catholic authorities believe that his bones are buried in the city of Santiago in northwestern Spain.

JOHN

Fortunately, we have a considerable amount of information about the disciple named John. Mark tells us he was the brother of James, son of Zebedee (Mark 1:19). Mark says that James and John worked with the "hired servants" of their father (Mark 1:20).

Some scholars speculate that John's mother was Salome, who observed the crucifixion of Jesus (Mark 15:40). If Salome was the sister of Jesus' mother, as the Gospel of John suggests (John 19:25), John may have been a cousin of Jesus.

Jesus found John and his brother James mending their nets

beside the Sea of Galilee. He ordered them to launch out into the lake and let down their nets to catch fish. They hauled in a tremendous catch—a miracle that convinced them of Jesus' power. "And when they had brought their ships to land, they forsook all, and followed him" (Luke 5:11). Simon Peter went with them.

John seems to have been an impulsive young man. Soon after he and James entered Jesus' inner circle of disciples, the Master labeled them "sons of thunder" (Mark 3:17). The disciples seemed to relegate John to a secondary place in their company. All of the Gospels mentioned John after his brother James; on most occasions, it seems, James was the spokesman for the two brothers. When Paul mentions John among the apostles at Jerusalem, he places John at the end of the list (Gal. 2:9).

John's emotions often erupted in his conversations with Jesus. On one occasion, John became upset because someone else was ministering in Jesus' name. "We forbade him," he told Jesus, "because he followeth not us" (Mark 9:38). Jesus replied, "Forbid him not . . . for he that is not against us is on our part" (Mark 9:39-40). On another occasion, James and John ambitiously suggested that they should be allowed to sit on Jesus' right hand in heaven. This idea antagonized the other disciples (Mark 10:35-41).

Yet John's boldness served him well at the time of Jesus' death and resurrection. John 18:15 tells us that John "was known unto the high priest." A Franciscan legend says that John's family supplied fish to the high priest's household.[2] This would have made him especially vulnerable to arrest when the high priest's guards apprehended Jesus. Nevertheless, John was the only apostle who dared to stand at the foot of the cross, and Jesus committed His mother into his care (John 19:26-27). When the disciples heard that Jesus' body was no longer in the tomb, John ran ahead of the others and reached the sepulcher first. However, he allowed Peter to enter the burial chamber ahead of him (John 20:1-4, 8).

If John indeed wrote the Fourth Gospel, the letters of John, and the Book of Revelation, he penned more of the New

Testament than any of the other apostles. We have no sound reason to doubt John's authorship of these books.

Tradition says that John cared for Jesus' mother while he was pastor of the congregation in Ephesus, and that she died there. Tertullian says that John was taken to Rome and "plunged into boiling oil, unhurt, and then exiled on an island." This was probably the island of Patmos, where the Book of Revelation was written. It is believed that John lived to an old age and that his body was returned to Ephesus for burial.

JUDAS (NOT ISCARIOT)

John refers to one of the disciples as "Judas, not Iscariot" (John 14:22). It is not easy to determine the identity of this man. Jerome dubbed him *Trionius*—"the man with three names."

The New Testament refers to several men by the name of Judas—Judas Iscariot (*see below*), Judas the brother of Jesus (Matt. 13:55; Mark 6:3), Judas of Galilee (Acts 5:37), and "Judas not Iscariot." Clearly, John wanted to avoid confusion when he referred to this man, especially because the other disciple named Judas had such a poor reputation.

Matthew refers to this man as Lebbeus, "whose surname was Thaddeus" (Matt. 10:3). Mark refers to him simply as Thaddeus (Mark 3:18). Luke refers to him as "Judas the son of James" (Luke 6:16; Acts 1:13). The KJV incorrectly translates Luke as saying that this man was the *brother* of James.

We are not sure who Thaddeus' father was. Some think he was James, the brother of Jesus—making Judas a nephew of Jesus. But this is not likely, for early church historians report that this James never married. Others think that his father was the apostle James, son of Zebedee. We cannot be certain.

William Steuart McBirnie suggests that the name Thaddeus was a diminutive form of *Theudas,* which comes from the Aramaic noun *tad,* meaning "breast." Thus, Thaddeus may have been a nickname that literally meant "one close to the breast" or "one beloved." McBirnie believes that the name Lebbeus may be derived from the Hebrew noun *leb*, which means "heart."[3]

The historian Eusebius says that Jesus once sent this disciple to King Abgar of Mesopotamia to pray for his healing. According to this story, Judas went to Abgar after Jesus' ascension to heaven, and he remained to preach in several cities of Mesopotamia.[4] Another tradition says that this disciple was murdered by magicians in the city of Suanir in Persia. It is said that they killed him with clubs and stones.

Catacomb fresco. Dating from A.D. 200–220, this fresco is one of the oldest catacomb paintings yet discovered. It depicts the events of John 21, when seven disciples (i.e., Peter, Thomas, Nathanael, the sons of Zebedee, and two other disciples) feasted on bread and fish.

JUDAS ISCARIOT

All of the Gospels place Judas Iscariot at the end of the list of Jesus' disciples. Undoubtedly this reflects Judas' ill repute as the betrayer of Jesus.

The Aramaic word *Iscariot* literally meant "man of Kerioth." Kerioth was a town near Hebron (Josh. 15:25). However, John tells us that Judas was the son of Simon (John 6:71).

If Judas indeed came from the town of Kerioth, he was the only Judean among Jesus' disciples. Judeans despised the people of Galilee as crude frontier settlers. This attitude may have alienated Judas Iscariot from the other disciples.

The Gospels do not tell us exactly when Jesus called Judas Iscariot to join His band of followers. Perhaps is was in the early days when Jesus called so many others (cf. Matt. 4:18-22).

Judas acted as the treasurer of the disciples, and on at least one occasion he manifested a penny-pinching attitude toward their work. When a woman named Mary came to pour rich ointment on the feet of Jesus, Judas complained, "Why was not this ointment sold for 300 pence, and given to the poor?" (John 12:5). John comments that Judas said this "not that he cared for the poor; but because he was a thief" (John 12:6).

As the disciples shared their last meal with Jesus, the Lord revealed that He knew He was about to be betrayed, and He singled out Judas as the culprit. He told Judas, "That thou doest, do quickly" (John 13:27). However, the other disciples did not suspect what Judas was about to do. John reports that "some of them thought, because Judas had the bag, that Jesus had said unto him, 'Buy those things that we have need of against the (Passover) feast . . .' " (John 13:28-29).

Scholars have offered several theories about the reason for Judas' betrayal. Some think that he was reacting to Jesus' rebuke when he criticized the woman with the ointment.[5] Others think that Judas acted out of greed for the money that Jesus' enemies offered him.[6] Luke and John simply say that Satan inspired Judas' actions (Luke 22:3; John 13:27).

Matthew tells us that Judas in remorse attempted to return the money to Jesus' captors: "And he cast down the pieces of silver in the temple, and departed, and went and hanged himself" (Matt. 27:5). A folk legend says that Judas hanged himself on a redbud tree, which is sometimes called the "Judas tree." In most modern works, Judas is portrayed as a zealot or extreme patriot who was disappointed at Jesus' failure to lead a mass movement or rebellion against Rome. There is, as yet, little evidence for this viewpoint.

MATTHEW

In Jesus' day, the Roman government collected several different taxes from the people of Palestine. Tolls for transporting goods by land or sea were collected by private tax collectors, who paid a fee to the Roman government for the right to assess these levies. The tax collectors made their profits by charging a higher toll than the law required. The licensed collectors often hired minor officials called *publicans* to do the actual work of collecting the tolls. The publicans extracted their own wages by charging a fraction more than their employer required. The disciple Matthew was a publican who collected tolls on the road between Damascus and Accho; his booth was located just outside the city of Capernaum and he may have also collected taxes from the fishermen for their catches.

Normally a publican charged 5 percent of the purchase price of normal trade items and up to 12.5 percent on luxury items. Matthew also collected taxes from fishermen who worked along the Sea of Galilee and boatmen who brought their goods from cities on the other side of the lake.

The Jews considered a tax collector's money to be unclean so they would never ask for change. If a Jewish man did not have the exact amount that the collector required, he borrowed from a friend. Jewish people despised the publicans as agents of the hated Roman Empire and the puppet Jewish king. Publicans were not allowed to testify in court, and they could not tithe their money to the temple. A good Jew would not even associate with publicans in private life (cf. Matt. 9:10-13).

Yet the Jews divided the tax collectors in two classes. First were the *gabbai*, who levied general agricultural taxes and census taxes from the people. The second group were the *mokhsa*, the officials who collected money from travelers. Most of the *mokhsa* were Jews, so they were despised as traitors to their own people. Matthew belonged to this class of tax collectors.

The Gospel of Matthew tells us that Jesus approached this unlikely disciple as he sat at his tax table one day. Jesus simply commanded Matthew to "follow me," and Matthew left his work to follow the Master (Matt. 9:9).

Apparently Matthew was fairly well-to-do, because he provided a banquet in his own house. "And there was a great company of publicans and of others that sat down with them" (Luke 5:29). The simple fact that Matthew owned his own house indicates that he was wealthier than the typical publican.

A tax collector. While the Romans controlled Palestine, they contracted local businessmen to collect taxes. These businessmen appointed scribes known as *publicans* to do the actual work of collecting the tax. The publicans levied more than the legal tax, keeping the excess for themselves and their employers. Roman law did not limit the amount that they could charge, so most publicans overtaxed the people to a painful degree. For this reason, Jewish observers were scandalized when Jesus called a publican named Matthew to become one of His disciples (Luke 5:27-31).

Chalice of Antioch. This large silver cup (19 cm. or 7½ in. high) was discovered in 1916 at Antioch. At first, many scholars thought this was the actual cup used at the Last Supper. However, subsequent study of the artwork on the cup leads authorities to believe it dates no later than the fourth or fifth centuries A.D. The plain metal lining may be a substitute for an original glass vessel. In 1954, Warner Brothers Studios produced a feature-length film about the story of this cup, entitled "The Silver Chalice," starring Paul Newman and Jack Palance.

Because of the nature of his work, we feel quite certain that Matthew knew how to read and write. Papyrus tax documents dating from about A.D. 100 indicate that the publicans were quite efficient with figures. (Instead of using the clumsy Roman numerals, they preferred the simpler Greek symbols.)

Matthew may have been related to the disciple James, since each of them is said to have been a "son of Alpheus" (Matt. 10:3; Mark 2:14). Luke sometimes uses the name Levi to refer to Matthew (cf. Luke 5:27-29). Thus some scholars believe that Matthew's name was Levi before he decided to follow Jesus, and that Jesus gave him the new name, which means "gift of God." Others suggest that Matthew was a member of the priestly tribe of Levi.

Even though a former publican had joined His ranks, Jesus did not soften His condemnation of the tax collectors. He ranked them with the harlots (cf. Matt. 21:31), and Matthew himself classes the publicans with sinners (Matt. 9:10).

Of all the Gospels, Matthew's has probably been the most influential. Second-century Christian literature quotes from the Gospel of Matthew more than from any other. The church fathers placed Matthew's Gospel at the beginning of the New Testament canon, probably because of the significance they attributed to it. Matthew's account emphasizes Jesus' fulfillment of Old Testament prophecy. It stresses that Jesus was the promised Messiah, who had come to redeem all mankind.

We do not know what happened to Matthew after the Day of Pentecost. In his *Book of Martyrs,* John Foxe stated that Matthew spent his last years preaching in Parthia and Ethiopia. Foxe says that Matthew was martyred in the city of Nadabah in A.D. 60. However, we do not know from what source Foxe got this information (other than from medieval Greek sources) and we cannot judge whether it is trustworthy.

PHILIP

John's Gospel is the only one to give us any detailed information about the disciple named Philip. (This Philip should not be confused with Philip the evangelist—cf. Acts 21:8.)

Jesus first met Philip at Bethany beyond the Jordan River (John 1:28, RSV). It is interesting to note that Jesus called Philip individually while He called most of the other disciples in pairs. Philip introduced Nathanael to Jesus (John 1:45-51), and Jesus also called Nathanael (or Nathanael Bartholomew) to be His disciple.

When 5,000 people gathered to hear Jesus, Philip asked his Lord how they would feed the crowd. "Two hundred pennyworth of bread is not sufficient for them, that every one of them may take a little," he said (John 6:7).

On another occasion, a group of Greek men came to Philip and asked him to introduce them to Jesus. Philip enlisted the help of Andrew and together they took the men to meet Him (John 12:20-22).

While the disciples ate their last meal with Jesus, Philip said, "Lord, show us the Father, and it sufficeth us" (John 14:8). Jesus responded that they had already seen the Father in Him.

These three brief glimpses are all that we see of Philip in the Gospels. The church has preserved many traditions about his later ministry and death. Some say that he preached in France; others that he preached in southern Russia, Asia Minor, or even India. In A.D. 194, Bishop Polycrates of Antioch wrote that "Philip, one of the twelve apostles, sleeps at Hierapolis." However, we have no firm evidence to support these claims.

SIMON PETER

The disciple named Simon Peter was a man of contrasts. At Caesarea Philippi, Jesus asked, "But whom say ye that I am?" Peter immediately replied, "Thou art the Christ, the Son of the living God" (Matt. 16:15-16). But seven verses later we read, "Then Peter took him, and began to rebuke him. . . ." Going from one extreme to another was characteristic of Peter.

When Jesus attempted to wash Peter's feet in the Upper Room, the intemperate disciple exclaimed, "Thou shalt never wash my feet." But when Jesus insisted, Peter said, "Lord, not my feet only, but also my hands and my head" (John 13:8-9).

On their last night together, Peter told Jesus, "Although all shall offend thee, yet will not I" (Mark 14:29). Yet within hours, Peter not only denied Jesus but cursed Him (Mark 14:71).

This volatile, unpredictable temperament often got Simon Peter into trouble. Yet the Holy Spirit would mold Peter into a stable, dynamic leader of the early church, a "rockman" (*Peter* means "rock") in every sense.

Where Is Peter Buried?

Roman Catholic tradition maintains that Peter is buried beneath the magnificent structure in Rome which bears his name—Saint Peter's Basilica. Although the New Testament does not report a visit of Peter to Rome, there is historical evidence that he spent at least part of the latter portion of his life there. There are also extrabiblical references (such as the Acts of Peter) and numerous references in the writings of second- and third-century church scholars which confirm that Peter died in Rome. Eusebius gives A.D. 68 as the approximate date of Peter's death.

The early Christian apologists Tertullian and Origen state that Peter was executed by crucifixion head-downwards in Rome. They say that he was one of thousands of Christians who died under Emperor Nero's persecution. In all probability, Peter was executed at the Neronian Gardens, where the estate of the Vatican is now located. According to Tertullian and Origen, Peter was buried nearby at the foot of Vatican Hill. Gaius of Rome (third century A.D.) mentions this grave.

It is said that Peter's remains were taken to a vault on the Appian Way when Emperor Valerian began his persecution of the Christians (A.D. 258). There his bones rested with those of Paul, safe from the emperor's threatened desecration of Christian burial grounds. Later, Peter's remains were returned to their original grave, and in about A.D. 325 Constantine erected a magnificent basilica over the location at the foot of Vatican Hill. This basilica was replaced by the present Saint Peter's Basilica in the sixteenth century.

For many centuries, Saint Peter's Basilica has been the most highly revered shrine in the Western world. Thousands of worshipers journey to Rome each year to pray over the spot where Peter is said to be buried. However, in recent years scholars have challenged the claim that Peter is buried beneath the basilica. Vatican archaeologists made several excavations in the early 1960s to investigate the centuries-old claim. They found a first-century Roman cemetery with one hastily dug grave that might have been Peter's. The Vatican researchers felt this was a reasonable conclusion.

Gaius wrote that the tombs of the apostles were close to the Vatican, on the road to Ostia; this suggests another possible site.

The New Testament writers used four different names in referring to Peter. One is the Hebrew name *Simeon* (Acts 15:14), which may mean "hearing." A second name was *Simon,* the Greek form of Simeon. A third name was *Cephas,* Aramaic for "rock." The fourth name was *Peter,* Greek for "rock"; the New Testament writers apply this name to the disciple more often than the other three.

When Jesus first met this man, He said, "Thou art Simon, the son of Jona: thou shalt be called Cephas" (John 1:42). Jonah was a Greek name meaning "dove" (cf. Matt. 16:17; John 21:15-17). Some modern translations render this name as "John."

Peter and his brother Andrew were fishermen on the Sea of Galilee (Matt. 4:18; Mark 1:16). He spoke with the accent of a

Galilean, and his mannerisms identified him as an uncouth native of the Galilean frontier (cf. Mark 14:70). His brother Andrew led him to Jesus (John 1:40-42).

While Jesus hung on the cross, Peter was probably among the group from Galilee that "stood afar off, beholding these things" (Luke 23:49). In 1 Peter 5:1 he wrote, "I . . . am also an elder, and a witness of the sufferings of Christ. . . ."

Simon Peter heads the list of apostles in each of the Gospel accounts, which suggests that the New Testament writers considered him to be the most significant of the Twelve. He did not write as much as John or Matthew, but he emerged as the most influential leader of the early church. Though 120 followers of Jesus received the Holy Spirit on the Day of Pentecost, the Scripture records the words of Peter (Acts 2:14-40). Peter suggested that the apostles find a replacement for Judas Iscariot (Acts 1:22). And he and John were the first disciples to perform a miracle after Pentecost, healing a lame man at the Beautiful Gate of Jerusalem (Acts 3:1-11).

The Book of Acts emphasizes the travels of Paul, yet Peter also traveled extensively. He visited Antioch (Gal. 2:21), Corinth (1 Cor. 1:11), and perhaps Rome. Eusebius states that Peter was crucified in Rome, probably during the reign of Nero.

St. Peter's Basilica. According to tradition, Peter was executed in the circus of Nero, where thousands of Christians suffered martyrdom. In A.D. 319, Emperor Constantine destroyed the circus and built over its northern foundations the first basilica of Saint Peter. The present structure was started in 1450 and took 178 years to build. Michelangelo designed the magnificent dome. St. Peter's is the largest church building in the world.

Peter felt free to minister to the Gentiles (cf. Acts 10) but he is best known as the apostle to the Jews (cf. Gal. 2:8). As Paul took a more active role in the work of the church and as the Jews became more hostile to Christianity, Peter faded into the background of the New Testament narrative.

The Roman Catholic church traces the authority of the Pope back to Peter, for it is alleged that Peter was bishop of the church at Rome when he died. Tradition says that the Basilica of St. Peter in Rome is built over the spot where Peter was buried. Modern excavations under the ancient church demonstrate a very old Roman cemetery and some graves hastily used for Christian burials. A careful reading of the Gospels and the early segment of Acts would tend to support the tradition that Peter was the leading figure of the early church. The tradition that Peter was the leading figure of the apostolic church has strong support.

SIMON ZELOTES

Matthew and Mark refer to a disciple named "Simon the Canaanite" (modern translations have "Canaanean," which is more correct), while Luke and the Book of Acts refer to one named "Simon Zelotes." These names refer to the same man. *Zelotes* is a Greek word that means "zealous one"; "Canaanite" is an English transliteration of the Aramaic word *kanna'ah*, which also means "zealous one"; thus it appears that this disciple belonged to the Jewish sect known as the Zealots. *(See* chapter 5, "Jews in New Testament Times.")

The Scripture does not indicate when Simon Zelotes was invited to join the apostles. Tradition says that Jesus called him at the same time that he called Andrew and Peter, James and John, Judas Iscariot and Thaddeus (cf. Matt. 4:18-22).

We have several conflicting stories about the later ministry of this man. The Coptic church of Egypt says that he preached in Egypt, Africa, Great Britain, and Persia; other early sources agree that he ministered in the British Isles but this is doubtful. Nicephorus of Constantinople wrote: "Simon

The Last Supper. Leonardo de Vinci (1452–1519) began work in 1496 on what many art critics consider to be his greatest masterpiece. Christ is shown at the center of the table. He has just revealed that one of them would betray Him. The disciples murmur among themselves, wondering which of them would do this (Luke 22:21-23). Judas, the second figure left of center, sits silently and clutches the disciples' purse (cf. John 12:4-6).

born in Cana of Galilee who . . . was surnamed Zelotes, having received the Holy Ghost from above, traveled through Egypt and Africa, then Mauretania and Libya, preaching the Gospel. And the same doctrine he taught to the Occidental Sea and the Isles called Britanniae."[7]

THOMAS

The Gospel of John gives us a more complete picture of the disciple named Thomas than we receive from the Synoptic Gospels or the Book of Acts. John tells us he was also called Didymus (John 20:4). The Greek word for "twins" just as the Hebrew word *t'hom* means "twin." The Latin Vulgate used Didymus as a proper name and that style was followed by most English versions until the twentieth century. The RSV and other recent translations refer to him as "Thomas called the Twin."

We do not know who Thomas might have been, nor do we know anything about his family background or how he was invited to join the apostles. However, we know that Thomas joined six other disciples who returned to the fishing boats after Jesus was crucified (John 21:2-3). This suggested that he may have learned the fishing trade as a young man.

On one occasion Jesus told His disciples that He intended to return to Judea. His disciples warned Him not to go because of the hostility toward Him there. But Thomas said, "Let us also go, that we may die with him" (John 11:16).

Yet modern readers often forget Thomas' courage; he is more often remembered for his weakness and doubt. In the Upper Room Jesus told His disciples, "Whither I go ye know, and the way ye know." But Thomas retorted, "Lord, we know not whither thou goest; and how can we know the way?" (John 14:4-5). After Jesus rose from the dead, Thomas told his friends, "Except I shall see in his hands the print of the nails, and put my finger into the print of the nails, and thrust my hand into his side, I will not believe" (John 20:25). A few days later Jesus appeared to Thomas and the other disciples to give them physical proof that He was alive. Then Thomas exclaimed, "My Lord and my God" (John 20:28).

The early church fathers respected the example of Thomas. Augustine commented, "He doubted that we might not doubt."

Tradition says that Thomas eventually became a missionary in India. It is said that he was martyred there and buried in Mylapore, now a suburb of Madras. His name is carried on by the very title of the Marthoma or "Master Thomas" church.

JUDAS' REPLACEMENT

Following the death of Judas Iscariot, Simon Peter suggested that the disciples choose someone to replace the betrayer. Peter's speech outlined certain qualifications for the new apostle (cf. Acts 1:15-22). The apostle had to know of Jesus "from the baptism of John, unto that same day that he was taken up from us." He also had to be a "witness with us of his resurrection" (Acts 1:22).

The apostles found two men who met the qualifications: Joseph surnamed Justus and Matthias (Acts 1:23). They cast lots to decide the matter and the lot fell to Matthias.

The name Matthias is a variant of the Hebrew name *Mattathias,* which means "gift of God." Unfortunately, Scripture tells us nothing about the ministry of Matthias. Eusebius speculated that Matthias would have been one of the seventy disciples that Jesus sent out on a preaching mission (cf. Luke 10:1-16). Some have identified him with Zaccheus (cf. Luke 19:2-8). One tradition says he preached to cannibals in Mesopotamia; another says he was stoned to death by the Jews. However, we have no evidence to support any of these stories.

Some scholars have suggested that Matthias was disqualified and the apostles chose James the brother of Jesus to take his place (cf. Gal. 1:19; 2:9). But there appear to have been more than twelve men thought of as apostles in the early church and Scripture gives us no indication that Matthias left the group.

8

THE EARLY CHURCH

The Greek word that English versions of the Bible translate as *church* is *ekklesia*, which comes from the Greek word *kaleo* ("I call" or "I summon"). In secular literature, the word *ekklesia* referred to any assembly of people, but in the New Testament the word has a more specialized meaning. Secular literature might use the word *ekklesia* to denote a riot, a political rally, an orgy, or a gathering for any other purpose. But the New Testament uses *ekklesia* to refer only to the gathering of Christian believers to worship Christ. This is why Bible translators render this word as *church* instead of using a more general term like *assembly* or *gathering*.

What is the church? What people comprise this "gathering"? What does Paul mean when he calls the church the "body of Christ"?

To answer these questions fully, we need to understand the social and historical context of the New Testament church. The early church sprang up at the crossroads of Hebrew and Hellenistic cultures. We have already surveyed these cultures in two earlier chapters, "Jews in New Testament Times" and "The Greeks."

In this chapter we turn our attention to the history of the early church itself. We will see what the early Christians understood their mission to be, and how unbelievers viewed them.

THE CHURCH IS FOUNDED

Forty days after His resurrection, Jesus gave final instructions to His disciples and ascended into heaven (Acts 1:1-11).

The disciples returned to Jerusalem and secluded themselves for several days of fasting and prayer, waiting for the Holy Spirit, whom Jesus said would come. About 120 of Jesus' followers waited in the group.

Fifty days after the Passover, on the Day of Pentecost, a sound like a mighty rushing wind filled the house where the group was meeting. Tongues of fire rested upon each of them, and they began speaking in languages other than their own as the Holy Spirit enabled them. Foreign visitors were surprised to hear the disciples speaking in their own languages. Some of them mocked the group, saying they must be drunk (Acts 2:13).

But Peter silenced the crowd and explained they were witnessing the outpouring of the Holy Spirit that the Old Testament prophets had predicted (Acts 2:16-21; cf. Joel 2:28-32). Some of the foreign observers asked what they must do to receive the Holy Spirit. Peter said, "Repent, and be baptized every one of you in the name of Jesus Christ for the remission of your sins and ye shall receive the gift of the Holy Ghost" (Acts 2:38). About 3,000 people accepted Christ as their Savior that day (Acts 2:41).

For several years Jerusalem was the center of the church. Many Jews believed that the followers of Jesus were just another sect of Judaism. They suspected that Christians were trying to start a new "mystery religion" around Jesus of Nazareth.

It is true that many of the early Christians continued to worship at the temple (cf. Acts 3:1) and some insisted that Gentile converts should be circumcised (cf. Acts 15). But Jewish leaders soon realized that the Christians were more than a sect. Jesus had told the Jews that God would make a New Covenant with people who were faithful to Him (Matt. 16:18); He had sealed this covenant with His own blood (Luke 22:20). So the early Christians boldly proclaimed that they had inherited the privileges that Israel once knew. They were not simply a part of Israel—they were the new Israel (Rev. 3:12; 21:2; cf. Matt. 26:28; Heb. 8:8; 9:15). "The Jewish leaders had a shuddering fear that this strange new teaching was no narrow Judaism, but merged the privilege of Israel in the high revelation of one Father of all men."[1]

A. The Jerusalem Community. The first Christians formed a close-knit community in Jerusalem after the Day of Pentecost. They expected Christ to return very soon.

The Christians in Jerusalem shared all of their material goods (Acts 2:44-45). Many sold their property and gave the proceeds to the church, which distributed these resources among the group (Acts 4:34-35).

The Christians of Jerusalem still went to the temple to pray (Acts 2:46), but they began sharing the Lord's Supper in their own homes (Acts 2:42-46). This symbolic meal reminded them of their New Covenant with God, which Jesus Christ had made by sacrificing His own body and blood.

God worked miracles of healing through these early Chris-

Amphitheater, Ephesus. Colonized by the Greeks around 1000 B.C., Ephesus enjoyed a long history as an important city of Asia Minor. It occupied a vast area with a population of more than one-third of a million. The city's theater could seat between 25,000 and 50,000 persons. Christianity probably came to Ephesus when Paul visited the city on his second missionary journey (Acts 18:18-19).

tians. Sick people gathered at the temple so that the apostles could touch them on their way to prayer (Acts 5:12-16). These miracles convinced many people that the Christians were truly serving God. Temple officials arrested the apostles in an effort to suppress the people's interest in the new religion. But God sent an angel to deliver the apostles from prison (Acts 5:17-20), which aroused more excitement.

The church grew so rapidly that the apostles had to appoint seven men to distribute goods to the needy widows. The leader of these men was Stephen, "a man full of faith and of the Holy Ghost" (Acts 6:5). Here we see the beginning of church government. The apostles had to delegate some of their duties to other leaders. As time passed, church offices were arranged in a rather complex structure.

B. The Murder of Stephen. One day a group of Jewish men seized Stephen and brought him before the council of the high priest, charging him with blasphemy. Stephen made an eloquent defense of the Christian faith, explaining how Jesus fulfilled the ancient prophecies of the Messiah who would deliver His people from the bondage of sin. He denounced the Jews as "betrayers and murderers" of God's Son (Acts 7:52). Looking up into heaven, he exclaimed that he saw Jesus standing at the right hand of God (Acts 7:55). This enraged the Jews, who carried him out of the city and stoned him to death (Acts 7:58-60).

This began a wave of persecution that drove many Christians out of Jerusalem (Acts 8:1). Some of these Christians settled among the Gentiles of Samaria, where they made many converts (Acts 8:5-8). They established congregations in several gentile cities, such as Antioch of Syria. At first the Christians hesitated to welcome Gentiles into the church, because they saw the church as a fulfillment of Jewish prophecy. Yet Christ had instructed His followers to "teach all nations, baptizing them in the name of the Father, and of the Son, and of the Holy Ghost" (Matt. 28:19). So the conversion of Gentiles was "only the fulfillment of the Lord's commission, and the natural result of all that had gone before. . . ."[2] Thus the murder of Stephen began an era of rapid expansion for the church.

MISSIONARY EFFORTS

Christ had established His church at the crossroads of the ancient world. Trade routes brought merchants and ambassadors through Palestine, where they came into contact with the gospel. Thus in the Book of Acts we see the conversion of officials from Rome (Acts 10:1-48), Ethiopia (Acts 8:26-40), and other lands.

Soon after Stephen's death the church began a systematic effort to carry the gospel to other nations. Peter visited the major cities of Palestine, preaching to both Jews and Gentiles. Others went to Phoenicia, Cyprus, and Antioch of Syria. Hearing that the gospel was well received in these areas, the church in Jerusalem sent Barnabas to encourage the new Christians in Antioch (Acts 11:22-23). Barnabas then went to Tarsus to find the young convert named Saul. Barnabas took Saul back to Antioch, where they taught in the church for over a year (Acts 11:26).

A prophet named Agabus predicted that the Roman Empire would suffer a great famine under Emperor Claudius. Herod Agrippa was persecuting the church in Jerusalem; he had already executed James the brother of Jesus, and had thrown Peter into prison (Acts 12:1-4). So the Christians in Antioch collected money to send to their friends in Jerusalem, and they dispatched Barnabas and Saul with the relief. Barnabas and Saul returned from Jerusalem with a young man named John Mark (Acts 12:25).

By this time, several evangelists had emerged within the church at Antioch so the congregation sent Barnabas and Saul on a missionary trip to Asia Minor (Acts 13-14). This was the first of three great missionary journeys that Saul (later known as Paul) made to carry the gospel to the far reaches of the Roman Empire. (*See* chapter 9, "Paul and His Journeys.")

The early Christian missionaries focused their teachings upon the Person and work of Jesus Christ. They declared that He was the sinless servant and Son of God who had given His life to atone for the sins of all people who put their trust in

Him (Rom. 5:8-10). He was the One whom God raised from the dead to defeat the powers of sin (Rom. 4:24-25; 1 Cor. 15:17).

CHURCH GOVERNMENT

At first, Jesus' followers saw no need to develop a system of church government. They expected Christ to return soon, so they dealt with internal problems as the need arose—usually in a very informal way.

But by the time Paul wrote his letters to the churches, Christians realized the need to organize their work. The New Testament does not give us a detailed picture of this early church government. Apparently, one or more elders *(presbyters)* presided over the affairs of each congregation (cf. Rom. 12:6-8; 1 Thess. 5:12; Heb. 13:7, 17, 24), just as elders did in Jewish synagogues. These elders were chosen by the Holy Spirit (Acts 20:20), yet apostles appointed them (Acts 14:13). Thus the Holy Spirit worked through the apostles to ordain leaders for the ministry. Some ministers called *evangelists* seem to have traveled from one congregation to another, as the apostles did. Their title means "men who handle the gospel." Some have thought they were all personal deputies of the apostles, as Timothy was of Paul; others suppose that they gained their name through manifesting a special gift of evangelism. The elders assumed the normal pastoral duties between the visits of these evangelists.

In some congregations, the elders appointed deacons to distribute food to the needy or care for other material needs (cf. 1 Tim. 3:12). The first deacons were the "men of honest report" that the elders of Jerusalem appointed to care for widows in the congregation (Acts 6:1-6).

Some New Testament letters refer to *bishops* in the early church. This is a bit confusing, since these "bishops" did not form an upper tier of church leadership as they do in some churches where the title is used today. Paul reminded the elders of Ephesus that they were bishops (Acts 20:28), and he seems to use the terms *elder* and *bishop* interchangeably (Titus 1:5-9). Both bishops and elders were charged with the oversight of a congregation. Apparently both terms refer to the same ministers in the early church, namely the presbyters.

Paul and the other apostles recognized that the Holy Spirit gave special leadership abilities to certain people (1 Cor. 12:28). So when they conferred an official title upon a Christian brother or sister, they were confirming what the Holy Spirit had already done.

There was no earthly center of power in the early church. The Christians understood that Christ was the center and source of all its powers (Acts 20:28). Ministry meant serving in humility, rather than ruling from a lofty office (cf. Matt. 20:26-28). By the time Paul wrote his pastoral epistles, Christians recognized the importance of preserving Christ's teachings through ministers who devoted themselves to special study, "rightly dividing the word of truth" (2 Tim. 2:15).

The early church did not offer magical powers to individuals through rituals or any other way. The Christians invited unbelievers into their group, the body of Christ (Eph. 1:23), which would be saved as a whole. The apostles and evangelists proclaimed that Christ would return for His people, "the bride of Christ" (cf. Rev. 21:2; 22:17). They denied that individuals could gain special powers from Christ for their own selfish ends (Acts 8:9-24; 13:7-12).

PATTERNS OF WORSHIP

As the early Christians worshiped together, they established patterns of worship that were quite different from the synagogue services. We have no clear picture of early Christian worship until A.D. 150, when Justin Martyr described typical worship services in his writings. We do know that the early Christians held their services on Sunday, the first day of the week. They called this "the Lord's Day" because it was the day that Christ rose from the dead. The first Christians met at the temple in Jerusalem, in synagogues, or in private homes (Acts 2:46; 13:14-16; 20:7-8). Some scholars believe that the reference to Paul's teaching in the school of "one Tyrannus" (Acts 19:9) indicates that the early Christians sometimes rented school buildings or other facilities.[3] We have no evidence that Christians built special facilities for their worship services for more than a century after the time of Christ. Where Christians were persecuted, they had to meet in secret places such as the *catacombs* (underground tombs) in Rome.

Scholars believe that the first Christians worshiped on Sunday evenings, and that their service centered on the Lord's Supper. But at some point the Christians began holding two worship services on Sunday as Justin Martyr describes—one in the early morning and one late in the afternoon. The hours were chosen for secrecy and for the sake of working people who could not attend worship services during the day.

A.   Order of Worship. Generally the early morning service was a time for praise, prayer, and preaching. The Christians' impromptu worship service on the Day of Pentecost suggests a pattern of worship that might have been generally used. First, Peter read from the Scriptures. Then he preached a sermon that applied the Scriptures to the worshipers' present situation (Acts 2:14-42). People who accepted Christ were baptized, following the example of Christ Himself. The worshipers shared songs, testimonies, or words of exhortation to complete the service (1 Cor. 14:26).

B.   The Lord's Supper. The early Christians ate the symbolic meal of the Lord's Supper to commemorate the Last Supper, in which Jesus and His disciples observed the traditional Jewish Passover feast. The themes of the two events were the same. In the Passover, Jews rejoiced that God had delivered them from their enemies and they looked expectantly to their future as God's children. In the Lord's Supper, Christians celebrated how Jesus had delivered them from sin and they expressed their hope for the day when Christ would return (1 Cor. 11:26).

At first, the Lord's Supper was an entire meal that Christians shared in their homes. Each guest brought a dish of food to the common table. The meal began with common prayer and the eating of small pieces from a single loaf of bread that represented Christ's broken body. The meal closed with another prayer and the sharing of a cup of wine, which represented Christ's shed blood.

Some people speculated that the Christians were participating in a secret rite when they observed the Lord's Supper, and they fabricated strange stories about these services. The Roman emperor Trajan outlawed such secret meetings in about A.D. 100. At that time Christians began observing the Lord's Supper during the morning worship service which was open to the public.

C. Baptism. Baptism was a common event of Christian worship in Paul's time (cf. Eph. 4:5). However, Christians were not the first to use baptism. Jews baptized their gentile converts, some Jewish sects practiced baptism as a symbol of purification, and John the Baptist made baptism an important part of his ministry. The New Testament does not say whether Jesus regularly baptized His converts, but on at least one occasion before John's imprisonment He was found baptizing. (It may, however, have been John's baptism that He was administering.) At any rate, the early Christians were baptized in Jesus' name following Jesus' example (cf. Mark 1:10; Gal. 3:27).

It appears that the early Christians interpreted the meaning of baptism in various ways—as a symbol of a person's death to sin (Rom. 6:4; Gal. 2:12), of the cleansing from sin (Acts 22:16; Eph. 5:26), and of the new life in Christ (Acts 2:41; Rom. 6:3). Occasionally the entire family of a new convert would be baptized (cf. Acts 11:16; 1 Cor. 1:16), which may have signified the person's desire to consecrate all that he had to Christ.

D. Church Calendar. The New Testament gives no evidence that the early church observed any holy days, other than holding its worship on the first day of the week (Acts 20:7; 1 Cor. 16:2; Rev. 1:10). The Christians did not observe Sunday as a day of rest until the fourth century A.D., when Emperor Constantine designated Sunday as a holy day for the

entire Roman Empire. The early Christians did not confuse
Sunday with the Jewish Sabbath, and they made no attempt to
apply Sabbath legislation to Sunday.

The historian Eusebius tells us that Christians celebrated
Easter from apostolic times; 1 Corinthians 5:6-8 may refer to
such a celebration. Tradition says that the early Christians
celebrated Easter at the time of Passover. Around A.D. 120, the
Roman Catholic church moved the celebration to the Sunday
after the Passover, while the Eastern Orthodox church continued to celebrate it at Passover.

NEW TESTAMENT CONCEPTS OF THE CHURCH

It is interesting to survey the various New Testament
concepts of the church. Scripture refers to the early Christians
as God's family and temple, as Christ's flock and bride, as salt,
as leaven, as fishermen, as a bulwark sustaining God's truth,
and in many other ways. The church was thought of as a
single worldwide fellowship of believers, of which each local
congregation was an outcrop and a sample. Early Christian
writers often referred to the church as the "body of Christ"

Isle of Patmos. The apostle
John received his vision of
God's judgment on this small,
rocky island off the south-
western coast of Asia Minor.
Tradition says that the Roman
emperor Domitian (A.D.
81–96) banished John to Patmos because he refused to
honor the state religion of
Rome. The Book of Revela-
tion confirms that the vision
was received on Patmos (Rev.
1:9), and seems to indicate he
wrote the book here (Rev.
1:11, 19; 10:4).

and the "new Israel." These two concepts reveal much of the early Christians' understanding of their mission in the world.

A. The Body of Christ. Paul describes the church as "one body in Christ" (Rom. 12:5) and "His body" (Eph. 1:23). In other words, the church encompasses in a single communion of divine life all those who are united to Christ by the Holy Spirit through faith. They share His resurrection (Rom. 6:8), and are both called and enabled to continue His ministry of serving and suffering to bless others (1 Cor. 12:14-26). They are bound together in a community to embody the kingdom of God in the world.

Because they were bound to other Christians, these people understood that what they did with their own bodies and abilities was very important (Rom. 12:14; 1 Cor. 6:13-19; 2 Cor. 5:10). They understood that the various races and classes become one in Christ (1 Cor. 12:3; Eph. 2:14-22), and must accept and love each other in a way that shows this to be so.

By describing the church as the body of Christ, the early Christians emphasized that Christ was head of the church (Eph. 5:25). He directed its actions and deserved any praise it received. All its power to worship and serve was His gift.

B. The New Israel. The early Christians identified themselves with Israel, God's chosen people. They believed that Jesus' coming and ministry fulfilled God's promise to the patriarchs (cf. Matt. 2:6; Luke 1:68; Acts 5:31), and they held that God had established a New Covenant with Jesus' followers (cf. 2 Cor. 3:6; Heb. 7:22; 9:15).

God, they held, had established His new Israel on the basis of personal salvation, rather than family descent. His church was a spiritual nation that transcended all cultural and national heritages. Anyone who placed his faith in God's New Covenant by surrendering his life to Christ became Abraham's spiritual descendant and as such a part of the "new Israel" (Matt. 8:11; Luke 13:28-30; Rom. 4:9-25; 11; Gal. 3–4; Heb. 11–12).

C. Common Characteristics. Some common qualities emerge from the many images of the church that we find in the New Testament. They all show that the church exists because God called it into being. Christ has commissioned His followers to carry on His work, and that is the church's reason for existence.

The various New Testament images of the church stress that the Holy Spirit empowers the church and determines its direction. Members of the church share a common task and common destiny under the Spirit's leading.

The church is an active, living entity. It participates in the affairs of this world, it exhibits the way of life that God intends for all people, and it proclaims God's Word for the present age. The spiritual unity and purity of the church stand in bold contrast to the enmity and corruption of the world. It is the church's responsibility in all the particular congregations in which it becomes visible to practice unity, love, and care in a way that shows that Christ truly lives in those who are members of His body, so that their life is His life in them.

NEW TESTAMENT DOCTRINES

The Bible sets forth the fundamental teachings of the Christian faith. The early church lived according to these doctrines and preserved them for us today. Let us focus our attention on how the New Testament presents Christianity.

A. Living in Christ. First of all, we are told that God the Father brings Christians into fellowship with Himself, as children in His family, through the death and risen life of Jesus Christ, the eternal Son of God. As Paul wrote, "God was in Christ reconciling the world unto himself" (2 Cor. 5:19). So the eternal Son took on human flesh. Jesus of Nazareth, fully God and fully man, revealed the Father to the world. The early Christians saw themselves as people "who through him are believers in God" (1 Pet. 1:21, NASV). They found new life in Jesus Christ and came into union with the living God through Him (Rom. 5:1).

Jesus promised that, by being "born again," men and women would find their proper relationship with God and savingly enter the kingdom of God (John 3:5-16; 14:6). The early Christians proclaimed this simple but startling message about Jesus.

Every major religion of the world has claimed that its "founder" had unique insight into the eternal truths of life. But Christians claim far more, for Jesus Himself told us that

---

Early Christian Hymns

It is impossible to determine what was the "first" Christian hymn. Christians adopted singing as an expression of thanksgiving or joy from the Jewish faith. Scripture tells us that Jesus sang a hymn with His disciples following the Last Supper (Mark 14:26); this most likely was Psalms 113-118, which were traditionally sung at the Passover celebration. The New Testament records other occasions when the apostles and other Christians sang. Paul and Silas, for example, prayed and sang hymns in the jail in Philippi (Acts 16:25).

What were these songs and hymns? It is impossible to say with certainty, but we find some fragments of these early songs throughout the New Testament. Ephesians 5:14 records part of what may have been a hymn of penitence:

"Awake thou that sleepest, and arise from the dead, and Christ shall give thee light." A hymn on the glory of martyrdom may have been the source of the saying in 2 Timothy 2:11-13: "For if we be dead with him, we shall also live with him . . ." Other examples are: Titus 3:4-7 on salvation; Revelation 22:17 on invitation; Philippians 2:6-11 on Christ as God's servant; and 1 Timothy 3:16 on Jesus' incarnation and triumph over death.

Besides serving as songs of praise, these songs were often intended to teach converts the basic truths of Christian faith and life.

Doxologies, or hymns praising God, were sung by early Christians and are recorded in fragments. For example, "Thou art worthy, O Lord, to receive glory and honor and power, for thou hast created all things, and for thy pleasure they are and were created" (Rev. 4:11).

Luke records a number of spontaneous songs that were so joyful they were often repeated by early Christians. These canticles have found their way into songs sung today. They include the "Magnificat," Mary's song of praise on learning she would give birth to the Savior (1:46-55); the "Benedictus," Zachariah's joy in the arrival of the Messiah (1:68-79); the "Gloria in Excelsis," the angels' song of praise to God (2:14); and the "Nunc Dimittis," Simeon's joyous thanks that the Savior has at last come (2:29-32).

Other early Christian hymns were written after the time the New Testament was written. "A Hymn to the Savior" is credited to the second century A.D. teacher and writer Clement. A literal translation of the first line of this song, which was included at the end of Clement's three-volume work about Christ entitled "The Tutor," is: "Bridle of Steeds Untamed." However, an English translation reads, "Shepherd of Tender Youth." This hymn uses numerous metaphors to describe Christ: Fisher of Souls, Everlasting Word, Eternal Light, and so on. This hymn instructed pagan converts on the nature of Christ.

"The Candlelighting Hymn," or "A Hymn for the Lighting of Lamps," was written at about the same time, though the exact date and authorship are unknown. We do know that second-century Christians gathered at dawn and again at twilight to sing hymns, and this hymn would certainly have been appropriate. This song is still used in the Greek Orthodox church as the vesper hymn.

He is the Truth, not just a teacher of the Truth (John 14:6). First-century Christians rejected the pagan religions and philosophies of their day to accept God's Word in the flesh.

B. Teaching Right Doctrine. The pagan religion of Rome was a rite rather than a doctrine. In effect, the emperor declared: "This you must do, but you can think as you please." Roman worshipers believed they needed only to perform the proper ceremonies of religion, whether they understood them or not. As far as they were concerned, a hypocritical skeptic could be just as "religious" as a true believer, so long as he offered sacrifice in the temple of the gods.

On the other hand, the early Christians insisted that both belief and behavior are vital, that the two go hand in hand. They took seriously Jesus' words that "true worshipers shall worship the Father in spirit and in truth" (John 4:23). What a Christian believed with his mind and felt in his heart, he would do with his hands. So the early Christians obeyed God (1 John 3:22-24), and they contradicted and opposed so-called Christians who tried to spread false teachings (cf. Tim. 6:3-5).

This is essentially what we mean when we speak of Christianity. It is a new life in Jesus Christ, which brings genuine obedience to His teachings.

Chapter 6, on "Jesus Christ," describes His teachings in detail. Here we will point out the basic differences between what Jesus and His followers taught and what their pagan neighbors taught.

1. The Doctrine of God. Nearly every major religion teaches that some Superior Being rules the universe, and that nature demonstrates this all-powerful Being at work. These religions often describe such a Being in terms of natural forces, like the wind and rain. But the early Christians did not look to nature for the truth about God; they looked to Christ. The Christians believed that Jesus fully revealed the heavenly Father (Col. 2:9). So they understood God in terms of Jesus, and they based their doctrine of God upon the life of Christ.

a. The Trinity. Many scholars believe the doctrine of the Trinity is the most crucial element in the Christian understanding of God. The early Christians confessed that they

knew God in three Persons—Father, Son, and Holy Spirit—
and these three fully share one divine nature.

Many scriptures show that these apostolic Christians understood Jesus Christ in trinitarian terms. For example, Paul said,
"Through him [Christ] we both have access by one Spirit unto
the Father" (Eph. 2:18)—describing our relation to the three
Persons of the Trinity. The New Testament contains many
statements like this.

In no way did the Christian doctrine of the Trinity agree
with the pagan teachings of the Egyptians, Greeks, and
Babylonians. Nor did it fit in with the abstract philosophies of
Greece. None of these ideas—religious or philosophical—
could compare with the Christian understanding of God, for
the early Christians knew that God was neither the capricious
hero of fictional legends nor an impersonal "Force" (1 Cor.
1:9). They knew He was a living personal Creator and Lord;
in fact, He came to them as three Persons. Yet He was still one
God.

b. God as a Personal Father. Jesus taught His disciples that
God is "My Father, and your Father" (John 20:17). In other
words, He showed them that God cared for them personally,
just as a human father cares for his children. He dared to
speak to God the Creator as a child speaks to his parent, and
He told His disciples God had given Him "all things" (Matt.
11:27).

Jesus explained that God loves the people who accept Him
(Jesus) into their lives (John 17:27). He reminded His followers that their Father-God cared for the smallest details of
their everyday needs (Matt. 6:28-32).

Jesus Christ taught that His Father is holy, and that He and
the Holy Spirit share the same divine holiness and act
accordingly (John 15:23-26). Unlike the gods of Greek and
Roman myths, who were short-tempered and immoral, the
true God is just and righteous (Luke 18:19). He intervenes to
save His people from sin. Jesus explained it was to this end
that God had sent Him into the world; He brought God's
mercy to a sinful and dying humanity, and in Him we see
God's holy purpose fulfilled (John 6:38-40). So this holy God

does not stand aloof from the affairs of men! He suffers their pain and even submits to the power of death to save His children (John 15:9-14). Again, we see Jesus emphasizing the personal love that God has for every human being.

Jesus demonstrated this love in His own ministry. He went out of His way to find people who were suffering from the effects of sin, so that He could deliver them. C. G. Montefiore says, "The rabbis welcomed a sinner in his repentance. But to *seek out* the sinner . . . was . . . something new in the religious history of Israel."[4] Jesus was willing to pay any price—even the price of death—to save mankind from the clutches of sin. In fact, when one of His disciples advised Him not to do it, He retorted, "Get thee behind me, Satan!" (Matt. 16:23). Jesus proved that God is the great Rescuer that the Old Testament prophets had described (cf. Isa. 53).

Jesus also broke down the narrow national limits that the Jews had erected around God. Jesus extended the love of God to all people, of all races and nationalities. He sent His disciples "into all the world" to win men back to God (Mark 16:15). The early Christians obeyed His command, carrying the gospel "to the Jew first, and also to the Greek" (Rom. 1:16).

2. The Doctrine of Redemption. Jesus taught that God redeems individuals as well as nations. This was a radically new thought in the Jewish world. Yet the doctrine of personal salvation was the heart of Christian teaching.

a. The Creator God. The Christian doctrine of salvation stood upon the fact that God created the human race. Even this was an unpopular idea in Jesus' day.

Many Greek philosophers and cultists insisted that God could not have made this evil world, and that it "emanated" from God by some natural process, as ripples "emanate" from a pebble dropped in a pond. But the Old Testament showed that God created the world on His own initiative. He chose to do it. And because God chose to create the world, He could deal with it in any way He wished (Isa. 40:28; cf. Rom. 1:20). Cultists taught that evil forces had distorted the "emanations" from God, making the world corrupt. The Bible teaches that

God created the world perfectly and made man in His own image, but man chose to rebel against God (Gen. 3). The Greeks believed that the forces of good and evil held the world in a stalemate; they thought evil had corrupted the good, and good kept evil from gaining absolute control of the world. The Christians rejected the idea; they taught that the world still belongs to its Creator, and that evil forces cannot finally prevail. Evil has only as much influence as God permits (Rom. 2:3-10; 12:17-21).

b. Fallen Man. Jesus gave the world a new understanding of man. His followers came to realize that each person is a lost child of God that the Father is trying to restore to the family through Christ (John 1:10-13; Eph. 2:19).

Greek myths said that man is a strange mixture of spirit and flesh, swept about by the unpredictable forces of the world. Orphic myths (stories involving the Greek god Orpheus) insisted that man had an inner nature like the gods. Plato had picked up this idea in his philosophy of the World-Soul; he

Claudius. Claudius, emperor of Rome from A.D. 41 to 54, had suffered an attack of infantile paralysis that left him with only partial control of his body. His slavering mouth, shaky limbs, and faltering gait gave him a weak appearance; but in reality he was one of the most ingenious and powerful of the Roman emperors. Claudius expelled the Jews from Rome for rioting; this is probably the incident referred to in Acts 18:2.

The Fate of the Seven Churches

Of the seven churches John addressed in the Book of Revelation, four now lie in ruin. The cities of Ephesus, Pergamum (or Pergamos), Sardis, and Laodicea are all desolate; but Smyrna, Thyatira, and Philadelphia still exist as modern cities.

When John wrote to Ephesus (Rev. 2:1-7), he warned the church of pagan influence and urged them to come back to their "first love." Ephesus was a large commercial center, often called "The Market of Asia." The temple of Artemis—one of the seven wonders of the ancient world—was located in Ephesus. In A.D. 262 the Goths destroyed the temple and the entire city of Ephesus. The city never regained its glory or its "first love." A group of Christian bishops held a council in Ephesus as late as A.D. 431, but Ephesus was later attacked by the Arabs, Turks, and finally the Mongols in 1403. Today the city's seaport is a marsh covered with reeds and the city itself is desolate.

In his message to Smyrna (Rev. 2:8-11), John praised the church for being a strong community of believers, but he warned that they would suffer persecution. From the time of John (ca. A.D. 90) until about A.D. 312, Christians were continually persecuted. In Smyrna the famous Christian martyr Polycarp was burned to death in A.D. 155. Smyrna was destroyed by an earthquake in A.D. 178, but was quickly rebuilt. Smyrna was one of the few Asian cities to withstand Turkish attacks, and among the last to fall to the Muslims. It was a cultural center, and its survival helped to spur the Renaissance. Smyrna is now the modern city of Izmir—one of Turkey's largest, with a population of half a million.

According to John, the Christians in Pergamum dwelt where "Satan's seat is." He warned that they would be swallowed up in this worldly city (Rev. 2:12-17). The capital city of the Roman province of Asia, Pergamum had magnificent statues of Zeus, Dionysus, and Athena. Christians there suffered, but in A.D. 312 Constantine became the emperor of Rome and ordered an end to Christian persecution. Later he professed Christianity and began molding church and state together. Pergamum became an important center of the state religion of Christianity. Attacked by the

---

felt that human beings had a spark of divine intelligence, and that man becomes more god-like as he develops his intellect and his ability to reason.

The Scriptures contradicted this Greek idea of man. They knew that the most important test of a man's character was his moral fiber, not his intellect; and in those terms, man certainly could not claim to be like God! "As it is written," Paul told the Roman Christians, "there is none righteous, no not one" (Rom. 3:10). The early Christians believed that, even though man is totally unworthy of God's love, God keeps on reaching out to man and trying to bring him back into holy fellowship with Him (Rom. 5:6-8).

The early Christian preachers spoke clearly of man's fall from God's favor in the Garden of Eden. "Death reigned from Adam," Paul wrote, ". . . even over them that had not sinned

Arabs in A.D. 716–717, Pergamum lost its political power. It gradually fell into ruin and is now a scene of desolation.

When John wrote the church in Thyatira (Rev. 2:18-29), he warned about worshiping false idols. There were no great statues of gods in the city, but trade guilds promoted idolatry and excessive drinking. The Arabs and Turks repeatedly attacked Thyatira throughout the years, but each time it was rebuilt. Because the new structures were erected over the ruins, the history of the city is difficult to trace. Now the city is a Turkish town of 50,000 called Akhisar, with little evidence of its character in the apostolic era.

John condemned the church at Sardis for having no life, no spirit (Rev. 3:1-6). After being destroyed by an earthquake in A.D. 117, Sardis was rebuilt by money provided by the Roman Empire. The city slowly lost its affluence, and was attacked and conquered by the Arabs in A.D. 716. There are some reports that Sardis was inhabited again after its destruction by Tamerlane (leader of the Berlas Turks) in 1403. Today a small village renamed Sart stands among the ruins of Sardis.

John praised the church at Philadelphia for its patience (Rev. 3:7-13). Philadelphia was located on a main geological fault line and was subject to frequent earthquakes, so the city was destroyed and rebuilt on several occasions. While the Turks and Muslims flooded across Asia Minor, Philadelphia long remained a Christian city; in fact, Philadelphia was the last Christian outpost in Asia Minor when it fell in 1390. It still stands as a modern Turkish town of 25,000 called Alashehir, meaning "City of God."

Laodicea was located on a trade route that made it a major banking center. By the fourth century, Laodicea had become the episcopal seat of Asia Minor and Christian bishops held a famous council there in A.D. 361. Laodicea's water supply was brought in from nearby cities by a sophisticated aqueduct system. Sunlight heated the water to lukewarm, which was the basis for the striking analogy in Revelation (Rev. 3:14-22). During the wars among the Muslims of the Middle Ages, Laodicea was destroyed and abandoned. By the seventeenth century, travelers noted that the city was inhabited only by wolves and foxes. Its ghostlike ruins remain desolate today.

after the similitude of Adam's transgression . . ." (Rom. 5:14). "For as in Adam all die, even so in Christ shall all be made alive" (1 Cor. 15:22; cf. 15:45). The Christians believed that Adam's sin in Eden was the first key event of human history. It meant that man was a fallen creature who needed to come back to God.

c. The Nature of Sin. Greek and Roman writers criticized the immorality of the ancient world, but they had no definite concept of sin. They feared that reckless living would destroy the harmony of their society, but in no way did they think immorality offended the gods. Why should they? According to their myths, the gods were more lustful and greedy than man would ever imagine.

Jesus taught that sin (defined in 1 John 3:4 as lawlessness) is rebellion against God; it is man's decision to abuse God's love and reject His way, and it brings judgment. ". . . For if ye believe not that I am he [i.e., the Redeemer], ye shall die in your sins" (John 8:24). Jesus predicted that the Holy Spirit would convict the world of sin "because they believe not on me" (John 16:9). Man chooses to sin, and he is fully responsible for his position in God's sight.

d. Jesus' Sacrificial Death. The Old Testament priests sacrificed animals and sprinkled their blood upon the altar for the people's sins. Jesus told His disciples that He would shed His blood "for the remission of sins" (Matt. 26:28). God Himself, in the person of Jesus Christ, was willing to give

Sardis. All that remains of the temple of Artemis (or Diana) at Sardis are a few magnificent columns. Once the wealthy capital of the Kingdom of Lydia, Sardis lay on an important trade route down the Hermus Valley. By the Roman period, the city had lost the prominence it had in earlier centuries. The letter to the church in Sardis (Rev. 3:1-6) suggests that the Christians there possessed the same spirit as the city, resting on their past without being concerned with present accomplishments.

Himself to die for man's sins. In this way, He bridged the gap that sin had opened between Him and man. The *incarnation* of the eternal Son of God enabled Him to be the final sacrifice for sin.

Jesus surrendered Himself to Jewish authorities who resented the message He brought to the world. They charged that He was "perverting the nation" by teaching His followers that He was the long-promised Messiah (Luke 23:2). Jesus had not broken any Roman law, but the Roman governor Pontius Pilate allowed his soldiers to execute Jesus to appease the Jewish leaders. So Jesus was not guilty of breaking God's law or man's; even His betrayer Judas Iscariot confessed, "I have sinned in that I have betrayed the innocent blood" (Matt. 27:4). Yet Roman centurions nailed Jesus to a cross as if He were a common criminal. In fact, He became God's pure sacrifice for the sin of man, and the early Christians emphasized this in their preaching and teaching (cf. Heb. 10).

e. Jesus' Resurrection. The Christians declared that Jesus' ministry did not end with the cross, because God raised Jesus from the tomb. He ministered among His disciples for several weeks until God took Him up to sit at His right hand in heaven (Acts 7:56).

The early Christians told the world how they had witnessed Jesus' death, resurrection, and ascension. This electrified the Roman Empire, and caused many people to regard the Christians as a group of fanatics (Acts 17:6). But Paul told his Christian friends, "If Christ be not raised, your faith is in vain: ye are yet in your sins. Then they also which are fallen asleep in Christ are perished" (1 Cor. 15:17-18).

3. The Kingdom of God. We have noted that Jesus focused upon God's salvation of the individual; but He also taught that God brings His people into a great community of the redeemed—the realm of God's saving sovereignty, which Jesus called "the Kingdom of God." In this Kingdom (presently expressed in the church), God required His people to live a life of brotherly love. They were to practice the ethics of Christ and work for the redemption of all mankind. Jesus did not limit the Kingdom to the Jews; He explained that everyone who was "bringing forth the fruits thereof" belonged to the Kingdom of God (Matt. 21:43). The Gospel of Matthew in particular records many *parables* (true-to-life illustrations) about the Kingdom; see especially Matthew 20:1-16; 22:2-14; 25:1-30.

Notice that many of these parables point to the end of time, when God will gather all the people of His eternal Kingdom to reign with Him forever. The early Christian evangelists stressed Jesus' message about the end of time, because they believed they lived in the last days. This spurred the Christians to take the gospel to the far corners of the Roman Empire. They had a burning desire to win lost souls for Jesus Christ before the end came.

9

PAUL AND HIS JOURNEYS

"He was a man little of stature," claims an account in the apocryphal second-century Acts of Paul, "partly bald, with crooked legs, of vigorous physique, with eyes set close together and nose somewhat hooked." If this statement is trustworthy, it tells a little more about this man from Tarsus who lived through nearly seven eventful decades after the birth of Jesus. It would fit Paul's own record of a taunt whispered against him in Corinth. "For his letters, say they, are weighty and powerful; but his bodily presence is weak, and his speech contemptible" (2 Cor. 10:10).

What he actually looked like will have to be left to the imagination of the artists—we cannot be sure. But more important matters press for attention—what he felt, what he thought, what he did.

We know what this man from Tarsus came to believe about the person and work of Christ, and other subjects crucial to Christian faith. Letters from his pen, preserved in the New Testament, bear eloquent testimony to the passion of his convictions and the power of his logic.

Here and there in these letters are bits of autobiography. Also, we find a broad outline of Paul's activities in the Acts of the Apostles, recorded by Luke, first-century gentile physician and historian.

So while the theologian has enough material to create endless debate about what Paul believed, the records for the historian are skimpy. A biographer of Paul soon discovers gaps in the apostle's life that cannot be spanned with anything more than a learned guess.

Like a flaming meteor, Paul flashes suddenly into view as an adult in a religious crisis, resolved by conversion. He disappears for many years, years of preparation. He reappears in the role of missionary statesman, and for a time we can trace his movements across the first-century horizon. Before his death, he flames on into the shadows beyond the limits of our straining eyes.

YOUNG SAUL

But before we can understand Paul, the Christian missionary to the Gentiles, it is necessary to spend some time with Saul of Tarsus, the young Pharisee. We find in Acts Paul's explanation of his identity: "I am a man which am a Jew of Tarsus, a city in Cilicia, a citizen of no mean city" (Acts 21:39). This gives us our first thread for weaving the background of Paul's life.

A. From the City of Tarsus. In the first century, Tarsus was the chief city of the province of Cilicia in the eastern part of Asia Minor. Although about 16 km. (10 mi.) inland, the city was a major port having access to the sea by way of the Cydnus River, which flowed through it.

Just to the north of Tarsus towered the lofty, snow-covered Taurus Mountains, which provided the timber that formed one of the principal objects of trade for Tarsian merchants. An important Roman road ran north out of the city and through a narrow defile in the mountains known as the "Cilician Gates." Many an ancient military struggle was fought at this mountain pass.

Tarsus was a frontier city, a meeting place for East and West, a crossroad for commerce that flowed in both directions by land and sea. Tarsus had a prized heritage. Fact and legend intermingled to make its citizens fiercely proud of its past.

The Roman general Mark Antony granted it the status of *libera civitas* ("free city") in 42 B.C. Thus, though part of a Roman province, it was self-governing, and not required to pay tribute to Rome. The democratic traditions of the Greek city-state had long been established in Paul's day.

In this city, young Saul grew up. In his writings, we find

reflections of sights and scenes in Tarsus when he was a lad. In sharp contrast with the rural illustrations of Jesus, the metaphors of Paul spring from city life.

The glint of the Mediterranean sun on Roman helmets and spears would have been a common sight in Tarsus when Paul was a boy. Perhaps this was the background for his illustration concerning Christian warfare, when he insisted that "the weapons of our warfare are not carnal, but mighty through God to the pulling down of strongholds" (2 Cor. 10:4).

Paul writes of "shipwreck" (1 Tim. 1:19), of the "potter" (Rom. 9:21), of being led in "triumph" by Christ (2 Cor. 2:14). He compares the "earthly tent" of this life with "a building of God, a house not made with hands, eternal in the heavens" (2 Cor. 5:1). He takes the Greek word that became *theater* in English and daringly applies it to the apostles, who "are made a spectacle *(theatro)* unto the world" (1 Cor. 4:9).

Miletus. The southernmost of the great Greek cities on the west coast of Asia Minor, Miletus flourished as a commercial center before it was destroyed by the Persians in 494 B.C. When Paul arrived here (Acts 20:15; 2 Tim. 4:20), it was part of the Roman province of Asia and declining commercially because its harbor was filling up with silt. Beyond the theater is the former harbor, now a marsh.

Paul's Method of Preaching

Paul was a persuasive preacher. His boyhood studies under Gamaliel had strengthened his Hebrew orthodoxy. Redirected by Jesus Christ, Paul exhorted his listeners to believe and be saved.

Paul pointed to his own life and work as proof of his message (2 Cor. 12:12). He heralded good news personally experienced (Phil. 3:12). He wrote, "For to me to live is Christ, and to die is gain" (Phil. 1:21).

Audiences found Paul frank, courageously zealous, poised and sympathetic. Paul reminded his Jewish listeners of their Hebrew history, language, and customs (Acts 13:14-43; 22:2; 23:6-9). Among Gentiles, he appealed to the Greek curiosity about new teachings (Acts 16:37; 17:22ff.). He compelled their attention with words, gestures, dramatic actions, and warnings (Acts 13:16, 40; 14:14-15).

Paul's one objective was to win men to Christ. His exhortations and warnings were warm and emotional (1 Cor. 15:58). He also used convincing arguments, well developed summaries (1 Cor. 10:31-33), and personal applications (Phil. 3:17; 1 Cor. 11:1).

Paul's preaching corresponded closely to Peter's pattern of preaching at Pentecost. Peter had projected five points: [1] "a man approved of God among you" (Acts 2:22) [2] "ye . . . have crucified and slain" (Acts 2:23) [3] "whom God hath raised up. . . . This Jesus hath God raised up" (Acts 2:24, 32). [4] "God hath made that same Jesus . . . both Lord and Christ" (Acts 2:36). [5] "Ye shall receive the gift of the Holy Ghost" (Acts 2:38).

Paul declared: [1] "God . . . chose our fathers . . . of this man's seed hath God raised unto Israel a Savior" (Acts 13:17, 23). [2] "Desired . . . that he should be slain" (Acts 13:28). [3] "God raised him from the dead . . . he was seen many days of them" (Acts 13:30-31). [4] "God hath fulfilled . . . unto us their children, in that he hath raised up Jesus" (Acts 13:33). Elsewhere, Paul reveals God's salvation for Gentiles (Acts 14:15-17; 17:22-31).

Paul reflected Jesus' teachings, although he seldom quoted Him. He preached with pastoral love and compassion. His message made many friends and some enemies, but allowed few compromisers. His theology centered in the person and work of Christ. He believed that the ethical demands of Jewish law were to be fulfilled; but he also believed that the new, Spirit-filled man performed from inward motivation what the law's demands had failed to achieve by force.

Such statements reflect the typical life of the city in which Paul spent the formative years of his boyhood. So the sights and sounds of this bustling seaport form a backdrop against which Paul's life and thought become more understandable. Small wonder that he should refer to Tarsus as "no mean city."

The philosophers of Tarsus were mostly Stoics. Stoic ideas, though essentially pagan, produced some of the noblest thinkers of the ancient world. The Tarsian Athenodorus is a splendid example.

When Athenodorus was retiring from public life in Rome to return to his native city, he gave this parting counsel to Augustus Caesar: "When you are angry, Caesar, say nothing and do nothing until you have repeated the letters of the alphabet." He is also credited with saying, "So live with men as if God saw you; so speak with God as if men were listening."

Though Athenodorus died in A.D. 7, when Saul was but a small boy, he long remained a hero in Tarsus. Young Saul could scarcely have escaped hearing something about him.

Just how much contact did young Saul have with this world of philosophy in Tarsus? We do not know; he has not told us. But the marks of wide education and contact with Greek learning are upon him as a grown man. He knew enough about such matters to plead the cause he represented before all sorts of men. He was also aware of the subtle dangers present in the speculative religious philosophies of the Greeks. "See to it that no one makes a prey of you by philosophy and empty deceit, according to human tradition . . . and not according to Christ," he warned the church at Colossae (Col. 2:8, RSV).

B. A Roman Citizen. Paul was not only "a citizen of no mean city," but a Roman citizen as well. This furnishes still another clue to his boyhood background.

Acts 22:24-29 shows Paul carrying on conversations with a Roman centurion and a Roman tribune (The *centurion* was a captain over 100 men in the Roman army; the *tribune* in this case would be a military commander.) On orders from the tribune, the centurion was about to have Paul scourged. But the Apostle protested, "Is it lawful for you to scourge a man that is a Roman [citizen], and uncondemned?" (Acts 22:25). The centurion carried the news to the tribune, who queried further. To him Paul not only affirmed his Roman citizenship but explained how he became one: "I was free born" (Acts 22:28). This implies that his father had been a Roman citizen.

Roman citizenship could be obtained in various ways. The tribune in the narrative states that he "bought" his citizenship "for a large sum" (Acts 22:28, RSV). More often, however, citizenship was a reward for some service of unusual distinction to the Roman Empire, or was granted when an individual was freed from slavery.

Roman citizenship was precious, for it carried special rights and privileges, such as exemption from certain forms of punishment. A Roman citizen could not be scourged or crucified.

However, the relationship of the Jews to Rome was not entirely a happy one. Jews rarely became Roman citizens. Most Jews who attained citizenship lived outside of Palestine.

C. Of Jewish Ancestry. We should also consider Paul's Jewish ancestry and the impact of his family's religious faith. He describes himself to the Christians at Philippi as "of the stock of Israel, of the tribe of Benjamin, a Hebrew of the Hebrews; as touching the law, a Pharisee" (Phil. 3:5). On another occasion, he called himself "an Israelite, of the seed of Abraham, of the tribe of Benjamin" (Rom. 11:1).

Thus Paul stood in a proud lineage reaching back to the father of his people, Abraham. From the tribe of Benjamin had come Israel's first king, Saul, after whom the boy of Tarsus was named.

The synagogue school helped Jewish parents pass on the religious heritage of Israel to their children. A boy began reading the Scriptures when he was but five years old. By the time he was ten, he would be studying the Mishnah with its involved interpretations of the Law. Thus, he became steeped in the history, customs, Scriptures, and language of his people. Paul's later vocabulary was strongly colored by the language of the Greek Septuagint, which was the Bible of Hellenistic Jews.

Of the major "parties" of the Jews, the Pharisees were the most strict (*See* chapter 5, "Jews in New Testament Times.") They were determined to resist the efforts of their Roman conquerors to impose new beliefs and ways of life upon them. By the first century, they had become the "spiritual aristocracy" of their people. Paul was a Pharisee, the "son of Pharisees" (Acts 23:6). Thus we can be certain that his religious training found its roots in loyalty to the regulations of the Law, as interpreted by the Jewish rabbis. At 13, he was expected to assume personal responsibility for obedience to that Law.

Saul of Tarsus spent his young manhood in Jerusalem "at

the feet of Gamaliel," where he was "taught according to the perfect manner of the law . . ." (Acts 22:3). Gamaliel was the grandson of Hillel, one of the greatest of the Jewish rabbis. The school of Hillel was the more liberal of the two major schools of thought among the Pharisees. Acts 5:33-39, RSV, gives a glimpse of Gamaliel, who is described as being "held in honor by all the people."

Rabbinic students were required to learn a trade so that they could eventually teach without becoming a burden to the people. Paul selected a typical Tarsian industry, making tents

Wall of Damascus. Saul of Tarsus, on his way to persecute the Christians of Damascus, was struck to earth and heard the heavenly voice as he neared this city (Acts 9:1-9). This is the traditional site along the wall of Damascus where Paul was lowered in a basket to escape persecution after preaching in the city's synagogues (Acts 9:23-25). Paul had returned to Damascus after a period of solitude in Arabia (Gal. 1:17).

from goats-hair cloth. His skill in this trade later proved a great boon to him in his missionary work.

Upon completion of his studies with Gamaliel, this young Pharisee probably returned to his home in Tarsus for a few years. We have no clear evidence that he met or knew Jesus during the Master's ministry in the flesh.

From Paul's own pen as well as from the Book of Acts, we learn that he then returned to Jerusalem and dedicated his energies to the persecution of Jews who accepted the teachings of Jesus the Nazarene. Paul could never quite forgive himself for the hate and violence that characterized his life during these years. "For I am the least of the apostles," he later wrote, ". . . because I persecuted the church of God" (1 Cor. 15:9). In other references, he brands himself as "a persecutor of the church" (Phil. 3:6), one who "persecuted the church of God, and wasted it" (Gal. 1:13).

An autobiographical reference in Paul's first letter to Timothy sheds some light on the question of how a man of such sensitive conscience could become involved in this violence against his own people. "I formerly blasphemed and persecuted and insulted him [Christ, represented by His people]; but I received mercy because I had acted ignorantly in unbelief" (1 Tim. 1:13, RSV). The history of religion is replete with examples of others who made the same mistake. In the same passage, Paul refers to himself as "the foremost of sinners" (1 Tim. 1:15, RSV), undoubtedly because he persecuted Christ Jesus and His followers.

D. The Death of Stephen. Had it not been for the way Stephen died (Acts 7:54-60), young Saul might have turned away unmoved from the stoning, at which he held the executioners' clothing. It would have seemed just another legal execution.

But as Stephen knelt and the martyring stones rained upon his defenseless head, he testified to his vision of Christ in glory and prayed, "Lord, lay not this sin to their charge" (Acts 7:60). Though this crisis launched Paul on his career as a hunter of heretics, it is natural to suppose that Stephen's words stayed with him so that he became "hunted" as well—hunted by conscience.

E. A Career of Persecution. The events that followed the martyrdom of Stephen do not make pleasant reading. The story is told in a breath, "Saul laid waste the church, and entering house after house, he dragged off men and women and committed them to prison" (Acts 8:3).

CONVERSION ON THE DAMASCUS ROAD

The persecution in Jerusalem actually scattered the seed of faith. Believers dispersed, and soon the new faith was being preached far and wide (cf. Acts 8:4). "Yet breathing out threatenings and slaughter against the disciples of the Lord" (Acts 9:1), Saul decided it was time to carry the campaign to some of the "foreign cities" in which the scattered disciples had lodged. The long arm of the Sanhedrin could reach to the farthest synagogue in the empire in matters of Jewish religion. At this time, the followers of Christ were still regarded as a heretical Jewish sect.

So Saul set out for Damascus, about 240 km. (150 mi.) away, armed with credentials that would empower him to bring "any of this way, whether they were men or women . . . bound to Jerusalem" (Acts 9:2).

What was in his mind as he tramped on, day after day, in the dust of the road and the burning heat of the sun? The intensely personal self-revelation of Romans 7:7-13 may give us a clue. Here we see a conscientious man's struggle to find peace through observing all the minute ramifications of the Law.

Did it free him? Paul's answer from experience was no. Instead it became an intolerable burden and strain. The influence of Saul's Hellenistic environment in Tarsus must not be overlooked as we try to find the reason for his inner frustration. After his return to Jerusalem, he must have found rigid Pharisaism galling, even though he professed to accept it wholeheartedly. He had breathed freer air most of his life, and he could not renounce the freedom to which he had become accustomed.

However, the deeper reason for his distress was spiritual. He had tried to keep the Law, but learned that he could not do so, by reason of his sinful fallen nature. How then could he ever be right with God?

With Damascus in sight, a momentous thing happened. In one blinding flash, Saul saw himself stripped of all pride and pretension, as the persecutor of God's Messiah and His people. Stephen had been right, and he was wrong. In the face of the living Christ, Saul capitulated. He heard a voice that said, "I am Jesus, whom thou persecutest. . . . Arise, and go into the city, and it shall be told thee what thou must do" (Acts 9:5-6). And Saul obeyed.

During his stay in the city, "He was three days without sight, and neither did eat nor drink" (Acts 9:9). A disciple at Damascus by the name of Ananias became a friend and counselor, a man not afraid to believe that Paul's[1] conversion had been genuine. Through his prayers, God restored Paul's sight.

EARLY MINISTRY

Paul began witnessing to his new-found faith in the synagogue at Damascus. The burden of his message concerning Jesus was, "He is the Son of God" (Acts 9:20). But Paul had bitter lessons to learn before he could emerge as a trusted and effective Christian leader. He discovered that people do not forget easily; a man's mistakes can haunt him for a long time, even after he has forsaken them. Paul was suspected by many of the disciples and hated by his former companions in persecution. He preached briefly in Damascus, went away to Arabia, and then returned to Damascus.

Paul's second attempt to preach in Damascus did not work out well, either. A year or two had elapsed since his conversion, but the Jews remembered how he had deserted his original mission to Damascus. Hatred against him flamed anew, and "the Jews took counsel to kill him" (Acts 9:23). The story of Paul's dramatic escape over the wall in a basket has captured the imagination of many a young lad.

Paul's days of preparation were not over. The Galatian account continues by saying. "After three years I went up to Jerusalem . . ." (Gal. 1:18). There he met the same hostile reception as at Damascus. Once more he had to flee.

Paul dropped from view for several years. These hidden years brought the ripened convictions and spiritual stature he would need for his ministry.

In Antioch, Gentiles were being converted to Christ. The church in Jerusalem had to decide how to care for these new converts. It was then that Barnabas remembered Paul and went to Tarsus to look for him (Acts 11:25). Barnabas had already been instrumental in introducing Paul to Jerusalem, in an effort to allay suspicions against him.

These two men were entrusted with the task of carrying relief funds back to Judea, where the followers of Jesus were suffering from a famine. When Barnabas and Paul returned to Antioch, mission accomplished, they brought young John Mark, Barnabas' nephew, with them (12:25).

MISSIONARY JOURNEYS

The thriving young church at Antioch now sent out Barnabas and Paul as missionaries. The first port of call on the first missionary journey was Salamis on the island of Cyprus, the home country of Barnabas. This fact, together with the Bible's frequent listing of these missionaries as "Barnabas and Saul," indicates that Paul was playing the lesser role. This was Barnabas' journey, Paul was second in command, and the two of them "had John [Mark] to assist them" (Acts 13:5, RSV).

The success of their missionary endeavors on that island fired Paul and his partners to press on into more difficult territory. They made a longer sea voyage, this time across to Perga on the mainland of Asia Minor. From there Paul meant to travel inland on a dangerous mission to Antioch in Pisidia.

But just at this point, something happened that was to cause much heartache for all three. The helper, John Mark, "departing from them returned to Jerusalem" (Acts 13:13), his home. We are not told why, though it is natural to guess that his courage and confidence had failed. Mark's sudden change of plans would later cause friction between Paul and Barnabas.

In Antioch, Paul became the spokesman and a familiar pattern developed. Some believed his message and rejoiced; others rejected his message and stirred up opposition. It happened first at Antioch, then at Iconium. At Lystra he was stoned and left for dead (Acts 14:19), but he survived to press on to one more city, Derbe.

The visit of Paul and Barnabas to Derbe completed their first journey. Soon Paul decided to retrace the difficult route over which he had come, in order to strengthen, encourage, and organize the Christian groups he and Barnabas had established.

In this we discern Paul's plan of planting congregations in the principal cities of the Roman Empire. He did not leave his converts unorganized and without suitable leadership; but by the same token, he did not remain long in one place.

The Jews often made converts among the Gentiles, but these gentile converts were kept in a "second-class" position. Unless they were ready to undergo circumcision and accept the Pharisaic interpretation of the Law, they remained on the fringes of the Jewish congregation. Even if they went that far, the fact that they were not born Jewish still barred them from complete fellowship.

So what would be the relationship of gentile converts to the Christian community? Paul and Barnabas journeyed to Jerusalem to confer with the leaders there regarding this fundamental issue.

At Jerusalem, Paul set forth his convictions and won the day. Paul's own description of the controversy in Galatians[2] states that he was given "the right hands of fellowship," along with Barnabas. The elders at Jerusalem agreed that these men "should go unto the heathen" (Gal. 2:9).

Following the conference in Jerusalem, Paul and Barnabas "continued in Antioch teaching and preaching the word of the Lord" (Acts 15:35). Here, two incidents put severe strains upon Paul's working relationships with Peter and Barnabas.

The first of these incidents arose out of the same problems that brought on the Jerusalem conference. The conference had freed Gentiles from the Jewish regulation of circumcision. However, it had not decided whether Christians of Jewish background could eat with gentile converts. Peter took his stand with Paul in this practice, which involved relaxing the Jewish food regulations. In fact, Peter set the example by eating with the Gentiles. But later he "withdrew and separated himself" (Gal. 2:12), and "Barnabas also was carried away with their dissimulation" (v. 13).

Paul, regarding these acts as a new threat to his mission to the Gentiles, resorted to drastic action. "I opposed [Peter] to his face, because he stood condemned" (Gal. 2:11, RSV). He did this "before them all" (v. 14). In other words, he resorted to public rebuke.

This incident helps us to understand the second, which Luke records in Acts 15:36-40. Barnabas wanted young Mark to accompany them on a second missionary journey; Paul opposed the idea. And the narrative says "there arose a sharp contention" (v. 39, RSV).

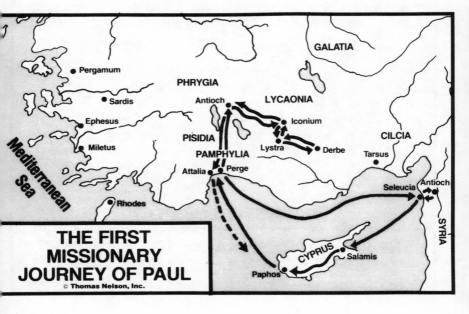

THE FIRST MISSIONARY JOURNEY OF PAUL
© Thomas Nelson, Inc.

We do not know whether Paul and Barnabas ever met again. They "agreed to disagree" and embarked on separate journeys. No doubt the gospel was thereby furthered more than it would have been had they stayed together.

Then "Paul chose Silas, and departed, . . . and he went through Syria and Cilicia, confirming the churches" (Acts 15:40-41). After revisiting Derbe, which had been the last point visited on the first journey, Paul and his company pressed on to Lystra to see their converts in that place. Here Paul found a young Christian named Timothy (Acts 16:1), and saw in him a potential replacement for Mark.

What happened here redeemed Paul from any charge of not being willing to place confidence in men younger than himself. In 1 Timothy 1:2, Paul addressed Timothy as "my own son," and in the second epistle he speaks of him as "my dearly beloved son" (2 Tim. 1:2). In the second epistle we also read, "I am reminded of your sincere faith, a faith that dwelt first in your grandmother Lois and your mother Eunice and now, I am sure, dwells in you" (2 Tim. 1:15, RSV). This

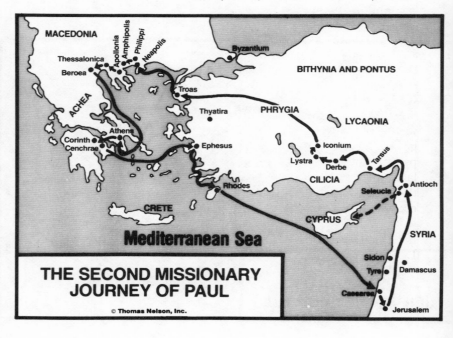

Street in Ephesus. Paul's words incited a mob of angry Ephesians to riot in the theater at the end of this marble street (Acts 19:21-41). Demetrius, who made small silver models of the great temple of Diana, stirred up the trouble when he found that Paul's preaching endangered his craft. Paul left the city, choosing Timothy to remain behind and prevent the church from being corrupted by false doctrine (1 Tim. 1:3).

reference may imply that Timothy's family had been won by Paul and Barnabas on their first journey. Certainly, when Paul came again, he "wanted Timothy to accompany him" (Acts 16:3, RSV). This same verse adds that Paul "took and circumcised him because of the Jews." Was this inconsistent with Paul's earlier judgment upon Peter? Or was it that he had learned the wisdom of not forcing unnecessary issues? At any rate, since Timothy was half-Jewish, this decision would avoid trouble many times. Paul knew how to fight for a principle and how to yield for expediency when no principle was at stake. Paul maintained that circumcision was not necessary to salvation (cf. Galatians), yet he was ready to circumcise a Christian Jew as a matter of expediency.

When the evangelistic party (directed in some unspecified way by the Holy Spirit—Acts 16:6-8) reached Troas and stood gazing across the narrow strait, they must have pondered the prospect of advancing their campaign to the European mainland. The decision came when "a vision appeared to Paul in the night; There stood a man of Macedonia . . . saying, Come over into Macedonia and help us" (Acts 16:9). Paul's response was immediate. The party set sail for Europe. Many writers have suggested that this "man of Macedonia" may have been Luke the physician. At any rate, he seems to enter the travel drama at this point, for now he begins referring to the missionaries as "we."

The journey continued along the great Roman road running westward through the principal cities of Macedonia—from Philippi to Thessalonica, and from Thessalonica to Berea. For three weeks, Paul spoke in the synagogue at Thessalonica; then he moved on to Athens, center of Greek learning and a "city wholly given to idolatry" (Acts 17:16). Restlessly, he journeyed on to Corinth.

His first major mission to the gentile world extended to almost three years. Then he turned back to Antioch.

After a short stay in Antioch, Paul set out on his third missionary journey in A.D. 52. This time his first stops were in Galatia and Phrygia. After visiting the churches in Derbe, Lystra, Iconium, and Antioch, he decided to do some intensive missionary work in Ephesus. Ephesus was the capital of

Old Appian Way. Paul traveled to Rome on this, the oldest and most famous highway in Italy (Acts 28:14-16). Appius Claudius began its construction in 312 B.C. Roman tombs, catacombs, and towering cypress trees line the way for many kilometers.

the Roman province of Asia. Strategically located for commerce, it was surpassed in size and importance only by Rome, Alexandria, and Antioch. As the outcome of Paul's labors there, it became the third most important city in the history of early Christianity—Jerusalem, Antioch, then Ephesus.

Paul came to Ephesus to undertake what proved to be the most extended and successful of his missionary efforts in any one locality. But these were strenuous years for him. Since he supported himself by working at his trade, his days were long. Following the custom of laborers in such a hot climate, he would be up and working at his trade before dawn. His afternoon hours were given to teaching and preaching, and likely his evening hours as well. He did this "daily" for "two years." In his own description of these labors, Paul adds that he not only taught in public, but "from house to house" (Acts 20:20). He succeeded—too well. We are told of "special miracles" (Acts 19:11) that took place during these stirring days in Ephesus. The new faith made such an impact on the city that "a number of those who practiced magic arts brought their books together and burned them" (Acts 19:19, RSV). This aroused the hatred of pagan worshipers, who feared that the Christians would undermine the influence of their religion.

After three winters in Ephesus, Paul spent the next one in Corinth, in line with the promise and hope expressed in 1 Corinthians 16:5-7. There Paul made further preparation for a visit to Rome. He penned a letter, telling the Christians in Rome, "I long to see you, . . . Ofttimes I purposed to come unto you" (Rom. 1:11, 13), and "I hope to see you in passing as I go to Spain" (Rom. 15:24, RSV).

Paul ignored warnings of the dangers that threatened him if he should appear in Jerusalem again. He felt that it was crucial that he return in person, bearing the gift of the gentile congregations. He was "ready not to be bound only, but also to die at Jerusalem for the name of the Lord Jesus" (Acts 21:13). So Paul came again to Jerusalem, and Luke writes that "the brethren received us gladly" (Acts 21:17). But lurking in the shadows was a reception committee with different intentions.

IMPRISONMENT AND TRIAL

The Christians in Jerusalem were happy to hear Paul's report of the spread of the Christian faith. However, some of the Jewish Christians doubted Paul's sincerity. To show his respect for Jewish tradition, Paul joined four men who were keeping a Nazarite vow at the temple. Some Jews from Asia seized Paul and falsely accused him of bringing Gentiles into the temple (Acts 21:27-29). The tribune of the Roman garrison took Paul into custody to prevent a riot. Upon learning that Paul was a Roman citizen, the tribune removed his chains and asked the Jews to convene the Sanhedrin to interrogate him.

Paul realized that the heated mob might send him to death. So he told the Sanhedrin that he had been arrested because he was a Pharisee and believed in the resurrection of the dead. This divided the Sanhedrin into its Pharisaic and Sadducean factions, and the Roman tribune had to rescue Paul again.

Hearing that the Jews were plotting an ambush for Paul, the tribune sent him by night to Caesarea, where he was guarded in Herod's palace. Paul spent two years under arrest there.

When Paul's Jewish accusers arrived, they charged that the apostle had tried to profane the temple and had created a civil riot in Jerusalem (Acts 24:1-9). The Roman procurator Felix demanded more evidence from the tribune in Jerusalem. But before new evidence could arrive, Felix was replaced by a new procurator, Porcius Festus. This new official asked for Paul's accusers to come to Caesarea again. When they arrived, Paul exercised his right as a Roman citizen to present his case to Caesar.

While waiting for the ship to Rome, Paul had an opportunity to plead his cause before King Agrippa II, who visited Festus. Acts 26 records Paul's speech, in which he recounted the events of his life up to that point.

Festus committed Paul to the charge of a centurion named Julius, who was taking a shipload of prisoners to the imperial city. After a very rough voyage, the ship was wrecked on the island of Melita (Malta). Three months later, Paul and the other prisoners boarded another ship for Rome.

The Christians of Rome traveled about thirty miles from the city to welcome Paul (Acts 28:15). Julius delivered Paul to "the captain of the guard" (Acts 28:16), who placed the apostle under house arrest. Acts 28:30 tells us that Paul rented a house for two years while waiting for Caesar to hear his case.

The New Testament gives us no account of Paul's death. Many modern scholars believe that Caesar freed Paul, and that the apostle engaged in more missionary work before being arrested a second time and executed.[3]

Two books written before A.D. 200—the First Epistle of Clement and the Acts of Paul—assert that this happened. They indicate that Paul was beheaded in Rome near the end of the reign of Emperor Nero (*ca.* A.D. 67).

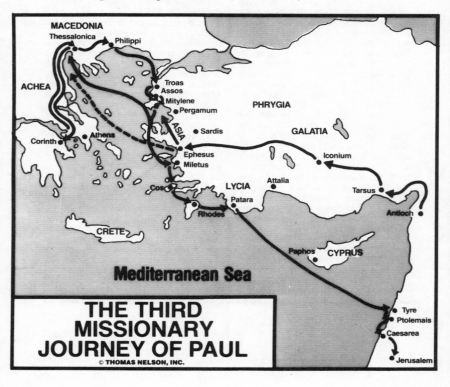

THE THIRD
MISSIONARY
JOURNEY OF PAUL
© THOMAS NELSON, INC.

New Testament Heretics

Since the first century, the church has been plagued by individuals who have tried to twist the truth to suit their own fancy or "refine" it to make it more acceptable or "sensible." Of special concern to the early church were three groups of heretics: Judaizers, Gnostics, and Nicolaitans.

Judaizers. At first the church was composed entirely of converted Jews who recognized that Jesus was the Messiah, God's Anointed One. But as Paul began his ministry among the Gentiles, some of the Jewish Christians warned that a Gentile could not become a Christian *unless* he or she first became a Jew! They said that the Gentile converts should practice physical rituals such as circumcision and adhere to the Law that Jews had kept for hundreds of years (Acts 15:1-31).

As Paul's ministry fanned out, it soon became apparent that Gentiles were flooding into the church with this Jewish indoctrination. Jewish Christian leaders followed in Paul's footsteps, demanding that the gentile believers conform to their beliefs. They used Old Testament Scriptures to support their point. At times these "Judaizers" even preceded Paul on his missionary journeys. In such cases, they caused so much turmoil that little or no evangelistic work could be done.

Gnostics. The Gnostics taught that Jesus wasn't really God's Son. To their minds, matter was evil and spirit was good. Since God was good (and spirit) He could not have personally created a material world (evil). They further argued that since spirit and matter could not intermingle, Christ and God could not have united in the person of Jesus. They took their name from the Greek word *gnosis* ("knowledge"), professing to have special insight into the secret truths of life.

Archaeologists have found several Gnostic papyrus manuscripts in Egypt. Some of them are pseudepigraphical writings, such as the "Wisdom of Jesus Christ" and the "Acts of Peter." Perhaps the best-known Gnostic book is the *Pistis Sophia* ("Faith Knowledge"), which has been translated into English and French.

Many small Gnostic communities were scattered across the Near East. Each developed unique doctrines of its own. Today we must rely on their manuscripts to trace the beliefs of each community, and in many cases it is difficult to tell whether a particular group was Gnostic or a totally different religious sect. A notable example is the community of scribes at Qumran.

Paul mentions three men who deserted the faith for this heresy: Hymenaeus, Alexander, and Philetus (1 Tim. 1:20; 2 Tim. 2:17-18). They claimed the resurrection had already passed, perhaps believing that whatever spirit is "left over" when a man dies is absorbed again into God.

Nicolaitans. John focused on a more extreme form of Gnosticism rampant throughout the first-century church (1 and 2 John; Rev. 2:6, 14, 15). These were the *Nicolaitans.* Supporters of this deadly doctrine claimed that, since their bodies were physical (and therefore evil), only what their spirits did was important. So they felt free to indulge in indiscriminate sexual relationships, to eat food which had been offered to idols, and to do anything they pleased with their bodies.

The early church dealt firmly with those who deviated from Christ's precious truths. They barred heretics from the fellowship and prayed for their salvation. Paul openly rebuked them. (Paul even turned against them at one point, when Peter refused to eat with gentile Christians in the presence of Jewish Christians—Gal. 2:12-15.) He felt that heretics had to be cut off from the church before they spread their ruinous ideas.

Irenaeus, Tertullian, and other church fathers denounced the Nicolaitans along with the Gnostics. Irenaeus reported that the sect was named for Nicolaos, a deacon of the first Nicolaitan community, who indulged in adultery.

PAUL'S PERSONALITY IN HIS LETTERS

Paul's epistles are the mirror of his soul. They reveal his inner motives, his deepest passions, his basic convictions. Without the surviving letters of Paul, he would be only a dim figure for us.

Paul was more interested in persons and what was happening to them than in literary formalities. As we read Paul's writings we note that his words may come tumbling out in hot

Amphitheater in Pergamum. The citizens of Pergamum (KJV, Pergamos) were the first to establish the worship of the Roman emperor, Augustus Caesar; John referred to the city as the "seat of Satan" (Rev. 2:13). It is located 80 km. (50 mi.) north of Smyrna in present-day Turkey. In the heart of the city the Greeks built this magnificent amphitheater with 78 rows of seats. Behind the row of columns was the Asclepieum, where the people of Pergamum worshiped the god of healing, Asclepias.

Gamaliel

Gamaliel is only mentioned twice in the New Testament (Acts 5:34; 22:3), but he may have exerted a more profound influence on the course of Christianity than these brief references indicate. He was one of the few Jewish leaders who earned the title of *Rabban* ("our master, our great one") rather then the ordinary title *Rabbi* ("my master"). Gamaliel held a respected place on the Sanhedrin, the governing body of the Jewish religion. The Jews' high esteem for Gamaliel is demonstrated by one rabbi's comment made upon his death: "When Rabban Gamaliel the Elder died, the glory of the Law ceased and purity and abstinence died."

We find clues to Gamaliel's influence upon Christianity in the two Scripture references to him. In the first instance (Acts 5:34), the Sanhedrin met in a specially called session to deal with the Christians, who insisted that the Sanhedrin was responsible for the Messiah's death. In this emotionally heated session, Gamaliel rose and asked that Peter and the other Christians be excused for a moment so that he could speak. When this was done, he proceeded with a surprisingly insightful speech that obviously swayed the Sanhedrin: "And now I say unto you, Refrain from these men, and let them alone: for if this counsel or this work be of men, it will come to nought: But if it be of God, you cannot overthrow it; lest haply ye be found even to fight against God!" (Acts 5:38-39). Rather than the flogging they anticipated, Peter and the apostles were given a severe warning and were released.

The second reference (Acts 22:3) was made by Paul, Gamaliel's former pupil. Paul was appealing to a Jewish mob, and he was not hesitant to link himself to this great teacher.

Gamaliel's greatness lay in his devotion to God and the Law. These incidents paint at least a partial portrait of his personality and Jewish tradition tells us that this elder statesman stressed the importance of repentance rather than of "works." Perhaps Paul's emphasis on this great Christian doctrine had its roots in Gamaliel's teaching.

Gamaliel's further influence on Paul can only be surmised. Surely Paul's great zeal—first for the Law, then for Christ—was captured from Gamaliel. Paul's love for the truth and his exhaustive understanding of the Scriptures might also be attributed to his teacher. With this training, anointed by the Holy Spirit, Paul built his New Testament treatises on the Christian faith, the church, justification, and regeneration. Paul's clear and logical manner of explaining the great doctrines of the Christian faith was no doubt the result, at least in part, of his schooling "at the feet of Gamaliel."

---

haste, as in the first chapter of Galatians. Sometimes he breaks off abruptly to plunge into a new line of thought. At points he draws a long breath and dictates a sentence almost without end.

Second Corinthians 10:10 gives a clue as to how Paul's letters were received and regarded. Even his enemies and critics acknowledged the impact of what he had to say, for they were known to comment, "His letters are weighty and powerful. . . ." (2 Cor. 10:10).

Strong leaders, such as Paul, tend to attract or repel those they seek to influence. Paul had both devoted followers and bitter enemies. Consequently, his contemporaries held widely differing opinions about him.

Paul's earliest writings antedate most of the four Gospels. They mirror him as a man of courage (2 Cor. 2:3), of integrity, and high motive (vv. 4-5), of humility (v. 6), and of gentleness (v. 7).

Paul knew how to differentiate between his own opinion and a "commandment of the Lord" (1 Cor. 7:25). He was humble enough to say "I think" on some matters (1 Cor. 7:40). He was very aware of the urgency of his commission (9:16-17), and of the fact that he was not beyond the danger of being "disqualified" through succumbing to temptation (1 Cor. 9:27, RSV). He recalls with sorrow that once he "persecuted the church of God" (15:9).

Street Scene, Nazareth.
Nazareth was a small city of low repute, yet Jesus' parents lived here and it became the boyhood home of the Savior (Luke 2:39-51). This narrow, winding alley of Nazareth looks much as the streets of Jesus' times would have appeared.

Read Romans 16 with special attention to Paul's generous attitude toward his co-laborers. He was a man who loved and appreciated people and prized the fellowship of the believers. In the Letter to the Colossians, we see how warm and friendly Paul could be, even with Christians whom he had not met. "I want you to know how greatly I strive for you . . . and for all who have not seen my face," he writes (Col. 2:1, RSV).

In the Colossian letter, we also read about a man named Onesimus, a runaway slave (Col. 2:10, 18) who had evidently added theft to the crime of forsaking his owner, Philemon. Now Paul had won him to the Christian faith and had persuaded him that he should return to his master. But knowing the severity of punishment meted out to runaway slaves, the apostle wanted to persuade Philemon to treat Onesimus as a brother. Here we see Paul the reconciler. He maneuvered to ensure a Christian welcome for Onesimus as he returned to Philemon. As we would say it today, he put Philemon "on the spot" in the eyes of the church and in terms of his personal relationship to Paul. And he did all this in behalf of a man on the bottom rung of the ladder in Roman society. Contrast this with the behavior of young Saul, guarding the garments of those who stoned Stephen. Observe how profoundly Paul had changed in his attitude toward persons.

In these writings we see Paul as a generous, warmhearted friend, a man of great faith and courage—even in the face of extreme circumstances. He was utterly committed to Christ, whether in life or death. His testimony is one deep anchorage in spiritual realities, "I know both how to be abased, and I know how to abound: every where and in all things I am instructed both to be full and to be hungry, both to abound and to suffer need. I can do all things through Christ which strengtheneth me" (Phil. 4:12-13).

FOOTNOTES

Chapter Three: *"The Greeks and Hellenism"*

[1]In later years, however, remnants of the Persian kingdoms would plague the eastern Roman Empire. The Parthians freed themselves from Greek control about 235 B.C. and wrested Persia from Seleucid control about 155 B.C. In about A.D. 225, a Persian named Ardashir overthrew the Parthians and set up the Sassanid kingdoms. These kingdoms became the cultural context for the rise of the Islamic religion.

[2]William M. Ramsay, *The Teaching of Paul in Terms of the Present Day* (London: Hodder and Stoughton, 1913), pp. 161–162.

Chapter Four: *"The Romans"*

[1]Will Durant, *The Story of Civilization:* Caesar and Christ. (New York: Simon & Schuster, 1944), p. 25.

Chapter Six: *"Jesus Christ"*

[1]Flavius Josephus, *Antiquities of the Jews* (Cambridge, Mass.: Harvard University Press, 1926), Bk. XVII, Chap. iii, Sect. 3. Some scholars think that Christians tampered with Josephus' account to show Jesus in a favorable light.

[3]Suetonius, *Nero* (New York: G.P. Putnam's Sons, 1935), p. 111.

[3]Tacitus, *Annals* (New York: Harper and Brothers, 1858), p. 423.

[4]Lucian, *The Passing of Peregrinus* (London: William Hernemann, Ltd., 1936), pp. 13, 15.

[5]At this point John's narrative seems to disagree with the Synoptic Gospels, which say that Jesus cleansed the temple at the *end* of His ministry. Some scholars believe He did this on both occasions. Others think that John relates the event in a different sequence to emphasize Jesus' authority.

Chapter Seven: *"The Apostles"*

[1]Edgar J. Goodspeed, *The Twelve* (Philadelphia: J. C. Winston Company, 1957), p. 99.

[2]H.V. Morton, *In the Steps of the Master* (New York: Dodd, Mead and Company, 1935).

[3]William Steuart McBirnie, *The Search for the Twelve Apostles* (Chicago: Tyndale House, 1973), p. 196.

[4]Eusebius, *The History of the Church* (Oxford: Penguin Classics, 1965), p. 65.

[5]*The New Westminster Dictionary of the Bible*, ed. by Henry Schneider Gehman (Philadelphia: Westminster Press, 1970) , p. 526.

[6]Karl Schmidt, "Judas Iscariot," *The New Schaff-Herzog Encyclopedia of Religious Knowledge,* Vol. 6, ed. by Samuel M. Jackson (Grand Rapids: Baker Books, 1977), p. 244.

[7]McBirnie, *The Search for the Twelve Apostles*, p. 213.

Chapter Eight: *"The Early Church"*

[1]Henry Melvill Gwatkin, *Early Church History*, Vol. I (London: Macmillan and Company, 1927), p. 18.

[2]Gwatkin, *Early Church History*, p. 56.

[3]Lars P. Qualben, *A History of the Christian Church* (New York: Thomas Nelson and Sons, 1964), p. 67.

[4]C. G. Montefiore, *Some Elements of the Religious Teaching of Jesus* (Folcroft, Pa.: Folcroft Library Editions, 1910), p. 57.

Chapter Nine: *"Paul and His Journeys"*

[1]Tradition says that God gave Saul the Hellenistic name Paul at the time of his conversion. Scripture does not say whether Saul adopted the name or whether it was given to him; nor does the Bible say when this change of name occurred. He is still called "Saul" during the time of his first missionary journey (Acts 13:19). But for the sake of convenience, we shall refer to him as "Paul" from this point.

[2]If indeed this is what the passage refers to; it may be describing an earlier visit to Jerusalem.

[3]*The New Westminster Dictionary of the Bible*, ed. by Henry S. Gehman (Philadelphia: Westminster Press, 1970), p. 721.

ACKNOWLEDGMENTS

The Publisher gratefully acknowledges the cooperation of these sources, whose illustrations appear in the present work.

P. Benoit, 179; Bildarchiv Photo Marburg, 52; British Museum, 38; Capitoline Museum, 42; Gaalyah Cornfeld, 106; J. Dupont, 16; Foreign Missions Board, 132, 191; Fototeca Unione, 67, 78; Ewing Galloway, 64, 68, 152; Giraudon (Paris), 7; L. H. Grollenberg, 199; The Hague, Kon Kab van Munten en Pennigen, 171; Instituto di Archeologia Cristiana, 142; Israel Government Office of Tourism, 79; Israel Government Press Office, 12; Levant Photo Service, 2, 56, 72, 83, 128; Matson Photo Service, 35, 183; Metropolitan Museum of Art, 146; Naples Museum, 51; Thomas Nelson, Inc., 89, 110, 150, 157, 197; Religious News Service, 164; Standard Publishing Company, 91, 96, 145; Willem Van de Poll, 20; Bastian Van Elderen, 174; William White, 76, 114, 118, 123.

The Publisher has attempted to observe the legal requirements with respect to the rights of the suppliers of photographic materials. Nevertheless, persons who have claims are invited to apply to the Publisher.

INDEX

This index is designed as a guide to proper names and other significant topics found in *The World of the New Testament*. Page numbers in italics indicate pages where a related illustration or sidebar appears. Headings in italics indicate the title of a book or some other important work of literature. Use the index to find related information in various articles.